The Camp Counselor

To
the increasing numbers of men and women, young and old,
who are awaking to the potential for the kingdom of God in
Christian camping, and who are willing to train themselves
to be useful camp counselors under the guidance of the One
of whom it is written, "His name shall be called Wonderful,
Counselor."

We see only what is,
God sees what is becoming.
Lord, as we serve campers,
Help us see like You.

The Camp Counselor

A guidepost to better Christian camping

Lloyd Mattson

Camping Guideposts
Duluth, Minnesota

Copyright 1981 by Lloyd Mattson. All rights reserved. Third printing, 1983

Published by Camping Guideposts, 5118 Glendale St., Duluth, Minnesota 55804. 218/525-3235

ISBN: 0-942684-02-8

Illustrations by Jeanne Mattson
Photographs courtesy of Camp Haluwasa, Hammonton, NJ

Printed in the United States of America

Contents

Foreword

There I was—a volunteer counselor at camp, enjoying the final campfire with two ten-year-old boys. They were twin brothers and both of them had invited Jesus into their lives that week. Friends in their town had paid their way to camp because their parents couldn't.

I'll never forget that night. As the other campers scampered off to their cabins, the three of us stood around the dancing fire. I prayed with them asking the Lord to be especially close as they returned to a difficult home situation.

After our amens I gave my little friends a hug and then Jimmy said it, "You kinda like us, don't you?"

That was powerful. And consequently, it's a delight to recommend a book that captures the dynamics of the counselor-camper relationship in Christian camping. Caring and loving counselors are the backbone of an effective, Christ-centered camping ministry. And *The Camp Counselor*, I predict, will be read, re-read, underlined, and greatly used by the vast army of camp counselors who have been hungry for training to be better prepared for God's work at camp.

Camp directors have been guilty too often of recruiting volunteer counselors by hook or crook, then tossing them into the cabin or canoe without benefit of training. "Just bring your tennis shoes, mosquito spray, and a Bible," they say. How much more comforting now to add, "And I'm going to mail you the *The Camp Counselor*—read it before you attend our pre-camp counselor training session."

Careful study of this book will help equip the camp counselor for the multi-dimensional role of father, mother, pastor, teacher, counselor, and friend to a cabin full of excited campers. With those responsibilities, a counselor needs all the help available! I especially appreciate the book's emphasis on helping campers grow spiritually, and the priority of following through on camper decisions. The camp counselor has a tremendous opportunity (and responsibility) in guiding campers toward spiritual maturity. Suggestions in this book will address the dilemma of decisions without disciples.

Lloyd Mattson writes the way the rest of us wish we could! His wisdom is rooted in scripture and has been tested on hundreds of wilderness trails, mountain climbs, canoe trips, and resident camp experiences in all sizes, shapes, and brands of camps. The counsel in this book is believable because Lloyd has tried it and refined it until it works. This is no ivory tower treatise, but a readable and workable counselor training book.

The Apostle Paul once wrote to young Timothy suggesting that he entrust the Gospel to faithful men who would in turn pass it on to others. I'm grateful for Lloyd Mattson's burning desire to help directors train camp counselors who in turn will win and train campers for Christ. *The Camp Counselor* will be an effective tool.

John Pearson
Executive Director
Christian Camping International

About This Book

Walk with me through the world of Christian camping. The *Camp Counselor* is a chat as we walk, a collection of stories and thoughts gathered from many places over quite a few years.

There are no camping authorities, you know. There are only observers and reporters. The best kind of camping is what works for you and the camp you serve. Christian camping is an art. The counselor is the artist. The camper is the medium in which the artist works. Since art flows more from the heart than the head, the *Camp Counselor* addresses the heart.

This counseling primer has been around in one form or another for some 20 years, surviving frequent revisions and printings. I have reworked this edition to reflect contemporary developments in camping. As with the first edition in 1962, the purpose is to provide evangelical Christian camps with a basic handbook for the beginning counselor.

How To Use The Book

Above all, read it! Read it thoughtfully, prayerfully, and purposefully. The value of any book lies more in what it causes the reader to think than in what it says. Read critically, for camping philosophy and procedure vary from place to place. Who is to say which way is best?

But before you read the chapters, turn to *Get Ready!*, the last section of the book. *Get Ready!* is a study guide. Review it carefully, noting the questions for each chapter. As you read the chapters, refer often to *Get Ready!*, marking the pages where answers are found.

You will discover that not all the information asked for in *Get Ready!* can be found in the *Camp Counselor*. Your camp must supply this. When no supplementary material is supplied, do the best you can from general information in the book.

The *Camp Counselor* spends little time on program detail—games, skills, stunts, campcraft, etc. This information is readily available. We focus on counseling principles and on the counseling spirit, seeking to stir the artist to his or her art. Prepare carefully, "for we are God's workmanship, created in Christ Jesus to do good works, which God prepared in advance for us to do" (Ephesians 2:10 NIV).

Lloyd Mattson
Duluth, Minnesota
1983

UNIT 1

The Counselor's Craft

The *Camp Counselor* is made up of three study units. The first unit provides an overview of the counselor's work. The second unit probes deeper into several topics introduced in Unit 1. The third unit presents resources for expanding the counselor's knowledge and skill, concluding with a self-study guide covering the book.

Unit 1

Chapter 1 discusses the counselor's personal preparation, concepts and attitudes that are important for serving children and youth in the camp setting. Foundations, tools, and camping objectives are reviewed.

Chapter 2 provides background on the history and development of Christian camping. We understand function better when we know something about the process that brought contemporary camping from its frontier setting to the present youth ministry.

Chapter 3 leads the counselor into the thick of the battle: life with the cabin group, expanding on themes introduced in the first chapter. Emphasis is placed on understanding the characteristics of age groups and coming to know individual campers. Experienced counselors will recognize that practices in camps vary widely, and that the chapter presents representative approaches to cabin-group life.

The fourth chapter moves beyond the counselor's primary responsibility for his or cabin group to participation in the overall camp program. The counselor is presented as a team member helping to fulfill the camp's objectives.

Chapter five moves into the cloudy areas of camping—unfavorable weather, health/safety procedures, special camper problems, and tragedy.

Chapter six brings the counselor and the individual camper together. No discussion in the book is of greater importance. The counselor's skill in meeting the needs of a single camper determines the value of the whole camping investment for that boy or girl.

Chapter seven finds the counselor staring at empty bunks and wondering where the week went! Camper evaluation, follow-up, camp evaluation, and self evaluation are discussed, concluding with a challenge to consider camping as a ministry for life.

1

The Trail to Camp

FORTY YEARS AGO on a chill dark night I vowed a solemn vow. Never again would I permit anybody to talk me into counseling at camp! I have renewed that vow two or three times each year since, usually on chill dark nights. Yet I keep returning to camp, even through pain is never far off. Few sorrows known to man have escaped me. Strange sounds in the night. Salt in my coffee. Canoe paddles and even a whole canoe spirited away! And that sudden illness at the far end of the cabin on a dark night, always coincidental with acute flashlight failure. I renew my vow.

Then in the morning some camper grants me the benediction of a shy smile, and my vow is forgotten. I expect I'll keeping on camping for as many years as the Lord grants strength; for life offers few joys to compare with this delightful business of camp counseling.

You can't succeed as a counselor unless you accept some misery along with the pleasure. Fair-weather counselors aren't worth much. But camp offers more sun than rain and more joy than pain. If you understand fairly well what Christian camping is all about, and learn well the role of a counselor, neither rain nor pain will discourage you permanently.

As a prelude to the study of camp counseling, let's follow a trail of introspection. Mastering the machinery of camping is of little value if a proper groundwork has not been laid in the heart. *Who* you are and what you are willing to become is infinitely more important than the skills you gain.

Take Uncle John Libke, a one-time street car conductor from Detroit. For many years he ministered to kids as counselor and Bible teacher. Uncle John didn't know much about archery or Ping-Pong, probably less about woodcraft. He just loved kids. When he paced up and down before his four-by-eight-foot flannel board telling Bible adventures, the campers sat straight and still. Who cared if Uncle John split an infinitive now and then?

When the story ended, Uncle John issued a simple invitation. "You who would like to talk about taking Jesus as Savior, come along," and Uncle John walked out. Three or four kids might follow; sometimes one, or none. But every heart respectfully followed Uncle John. Night and day he moved about the camp, enjoying the company of campers.

Right now, out there somewhere, are eight or ten kids who are concerned about one big problem. They plan to go to camp, and they wonder who will be their counselor. They are wondering about you!

Those kids will come from all kinds of homes. They will bring all manner of challenges to your cabin. You, more than anyone else, will determine what camp will be like. Will it be just another fun time with peaks and valleys? Or will camp be a launching pad, thrusting some into a spiritual trajectory higher than you can imagine? It's rather frightening to consider how much depends on you.

Ted Stockfish was reporting to our men's class one Sunday on his week at junior camp. Ted was aglow. "Man, what a week! In every cabin where we had a solid counselor, boys were saved." Then the glow faded. "But in some cabins, bad news." There were tears in Ted's eyes. The counselors made the difference.

Good counselors always seem in short supply. My prayer in writing this book is that you will accept this calling from God and become a good counselor.

Let's look at three foundations for effective counseling. Then we'll examine God's purpose for Christian camping, and see how that purpose includes the counselor.

Foundations For Effective Counseling

Three adults surrounded Millie in a corner of the darkened chapel; the camp director, the camp pastor, and Millie's counselor. The topic was ten dollars which had turned up missing in Millie's cabin just before she had suddenly displayed a burst of philanthropy.

Tears streaked twelve-year-old Millie's face. She shivered in her thin, faded dress. No, she hadn't stolen the money! Her aunt sent it in the mail. But Millie had not received a letter all week. Well it wasn't in the *mail*, but a letter a friend had left when she visited. Millie couldn't remember where her aunt lived, certainly not her phone number, or even exactly when the friend had visited. Finally Millie admitted lying, because she knew no one would believe she had found the money down by the beach. What time? Where?

The camp pastor applied theology, warning Millie of the consequences of unconfessed sin. The camp director tried psychology, assuring Millie full forgiveness if she confessed. Then Millie's counselor overflowed with compassion. She drew Millie close and whispered, "Millie, we love you."

A little love beats theology and psychology any day. Millie wept her confession. It was a familiar, sad story—a foster child without friends or money, a sister camper ignoring the rule about cash in the cabin, the euphoria of buying treats and friendship. Millie desperately needed love and acceptance. A counselor supplied that love.

There are many qualities that combine to make a good counselor, but here are three foundational check points. See how you measure up.

ENJOY YOUR CAMPERS

Kathy Nicoll, a veteran Canadian camp leader, once pointed out a common confusion among camping people. She spoke of adults who talk piously about *loving* kids, but who give every evidence that they didn't enjoy being with kids! There's a difference between loving and enjoying.

If a cabin full of kids unnerves you, then perhaps some other camp job would best meet your needs—and the campers'! A counselor's hidden fear or hostility outshouts the finest smiling speech. Working with young people always brings a certain amount of risk, but enjoying youth is a primary requisite for effective counseling.

Being able to enjoy campers doesn't mean there will never be a chill dark night! All who spend a few years counseling kids have hard times. But basically, if you enjoy youth and feel comfortable with them, you know that the sun will shine again.

Enjoying campers does not require that you abandon adulthood. Campers don't want a buddy, but a counselor. What sounds more silly than an adult salting his talk with the latest youth jargon? While remaining thoroughly adult, you can provide the atmosphere that makes for happy campers.

SURRENDER SELF-INTEREST

How many push-ups you can perform has little to do with counseling. Neither has marksmanship or the mastery of woodlore. Too many counselors exploit campers as a captive audience. *Camp is for campers!*

Surrendering self-interests means that you manage yourself for the well-being of your campers. Your only rights are those essential to maintaining health and mental equilibrium. The camp director should provide counselors with occasional islands of peace, but only when the campers are under the care of other staff persons.

This camping foundation creates problems because the kind of persons who volunteer for counseling often bring broad interests to camp. They are gregarious, hence the temptation to socialize with other staff persons at the expense of campers. Often they are competitive, with an urge to play rather than teach campers to play.

Many campers have been afflicted with the fisherman counselor, an unfortunate blend. Fishermen, ordinarily persons of integrity and high purpose, often suffer the compulsion of an addict. The sternest self-discipline must be imposed to avoid rowing off with two or three campers who must spend the afternoon watching the counselor fish. Teaching campers how to fish surely is a noble form of education, but let the counselor lock his personal tackle in the car!

A certain scoutmaster, it is reported, served faithfully for forty years. He built the best fires and pitched the trimmest tents; he cooked the finest meals and tied the strongest knots. Then he died. And they say the boys haven't been bored since.

Surrendering self-interest becomes more difficult toward the close of camp when the counselor's energies lag noticeably behind the campers.' But few people have died from lack of sleep, and much mischief is wrought during a counselor's clandestine nap, so keep alert.

A general rule holds that counselors should seldom do anything campers are capable of doing for themselves, either work or play. Campers deserve every learning and growth experience camp can afford. Watching a camper grow as he or she masters new skills is one of the counselor's rewards.

ACCEPT PERSONAL ACCOUNTABILITY

Come what may, you are responsible for fulfilling the camp's objectives in your campers. When a camper fails to achieve those objectives, the counselor has failed in some measure.

Sometimes you must compensate for another leader's weakness, or a bad day in the kitchen, or a solid week of rain. That's a tall order! Developing contingency plans strengthens your probability for success.

And sometimes you will fail. Several times I have been forced to send a camper home. I lacked the perception to redirect unacceptable attitudes. I lost him. This is the ultimate failure. What more might I have done? I don't know. In my judgment the camper had to go home to protect those who remained. Perhaps another time I will have better insights, like Millie's counselor.

Personal accountability suggests goals by which to measure success. One goal is *fun*. Camp must be fun, else why come? A man challenged me on this in a workshop one day. He pounded the table and growled. "We don't send kids to camp to have *fun!*"

I understood. This man felt a Christian camp should seek *spiritual* results; conversions, dedications, and commitments to missionary service. What place had *fun* in the grim business of escaping hell?

But youth's eschatology is somewhat limited. Campers seem more taken with the joy of the Lord. If camp isn't fun, they won't be back. Accountability requires that camp be as much fun as possible.

Of course spiritual gains are not alien to fun. Pleasant days create a spiritually receptive mood. Personal encounters with God for every camper make up the major camp goal; and such encounters are a part of all lesser goals; good food, adequate facilities, competent leadership, and fun.

Your accountability holds eternal consequences. It is possible that each year camp produces more significant spiritual decisions than any other church-related activity. Another chapter will discuss some of the reasons for this, but now we simply recognize the fact. Your task is to provide the best possible setting for each of your campers to hear God speak.

You may be asked to write a report on each camper, evaluating his response to camp. This demands careful observation and records to provide information for follow-up. But there is that other record, the accurate one kept by God. Leading campers to Christ is the crowning measure of accountability.

Accountability presumes a willingness to prepare thoroughly. While nothing mysterious or difficult surrounds the role of camp counseling, a great deal of information must be assimilated, and possibly some new skills must be mastered, if you are to help your campers gain full value from camp.

Having learned the fundamentals of the task, the best way to refine your knowledge is to practice personal godliness. Most counseling techniques are simply common sense; applying love, patience, humility, and the constant openness of spirit that all effective workers with youth must possess.

This book will give you the camping experiences of others. Beyond what common sense provides and what you can learn from others, you will encounter the quiet working of God. Your final accountability is to Him.

These then are foundations for effective counseling: enjoying your campers, surrendering self-interests, and accepting personal accountability. Since God has called you, you can trust Him to equip you for the work.

TOOLS FOR CAMP COUNSELING

Collecting a hundred kids in assorted buildings by a lake does not constitute Christian camping. Organizing cabin groups under responsible counselors still falls short. There are certain relationships and procedures, tested through more than a century of Christian youth camping, which promise spiritual success. Here are the tools you must work with.

YOU!

Beginning counselors sometimes imagine that a bag of skits, stunts, and rainy-day games assures success. Would it were so! But there is only you. You are unique, a gift from God to the world, with a blend of capabilities possessed by no other. You must be yourself to succeed; just yourself. You will of course work on any negative characteristics such as laziness (which we all share), undue modesty (not nearly as common), or an evil temper. Every Christian must manage himself as God's steward. In camp you are the basic tool in the counselor's kit.

The impact of camp is not program or facilities, but people. Some fit comfortably into the counselor's role; others belong elsewhere; for long after games and adventure are forgotten, campers remember their counselor.

A middle-aged minister once counseled a young man through several years of Bible camp. The minister played ball with him. He scolded him when necessary. He guided him in devotions and gave much time just to chatting. He encouraged the resolve he saw in the young man to pursue the Christian ministry.

One August afternoon the phone rang in a gas station where the young man worked. "Lloyd? I was just thinking about you. How is it with your soul?"

"Fine, just fine!" I replied. "Everything's fine." At that mo-

ment everything became fine, though in the days and weeks
before that call nothing had been fine. It is very probable that I
am struggling with a sentence at my typewriter this moment
because a camp counselor cared enough to phone. Yet before
he could touch my life through a brief, miraculously-timed
phone conversation, he had prepared the way by being a man
of God at camp.

CABIN ATMOSPHERE

Out of your personal life and preparation will emerge this
second counselor's tool. The impact of the small group on the
individual is gaining increasing attention. Camp leaders have
known about this all along. Helping cabinmates relate warmly
to one another creates the spirit that builds a great camp.

Not everything that goes on in camp will be shared as a
cabin group. But several times every day that group comes
together, and each evening comes that cherished—or dread-
ed—moment—lights out! It is a mistake to program the camp
so strenuously that no relaxed moments remain for the counselor and the cabin group. A proper cabin atmosphere relieves
the dread of lights out.

Many unrelated stimuli attack the camper's mind each day:
encounters on the ball field, tensions in craft class when something goes wrong, squabbles with another camper, lessons in
Bible class, chapel sermons. The sorting and absorbing of values await a reflective moment when the camper's heart and
mind react. Often you will hear campers say, "I was lying on
my bunk thinking about what you said, and . . . "

Later on we will outline details for cabin activity and discover ways to build that wholesome spirit so essential to
achieving camp goals. It is a vital tool in your kit.

CAMP PROGRAM

If more counselors understood this tool, their work would
be less taxing. Your assignment requires that you do all in
your power to relate each camper to as much of the camp as
he or she can absorb. This will fill camp hours to overflowing.

This tool contains the secret of all good camps. If the counselor does not understand it, campers will gain little from much that awaits them on the campsite. Young campers, especially, need encouragement to enter into activities. A wise counselor can motivate the shy camper. Recognition of a craft, even though inexpertly done, could be the highlight of the week for one of your campers.

Moving helpfully among campers throughout the day establishes friendship that prepare the way for pleasant cabin-centered moments. Knowing the content of a chapel message or Bible class provides a natural opening for cabin devotions. The camp program is a tool to be utilized carefully, for it provides the counselor with daily opportunities to demonstrate the spiritual principles taught in class and chapel.

CABIN DEVOTIONS

Much more thought needs to be given to the counselor's role in shaping the devotional life of campers. A later chapter will discuss one approach to this—a correlated Bible study and devotional plan that incorporates the key elements of personal Bible study and worship. Too often the cabin devotions at the close of the day fail to consider all that the campers have already absorbed. The notion seems to prevail that the more ideas put forth, the more learning takes place. But it is truth *grasped*, not set forth, that changes lives. Spiritual truth must be perceived by the spirit, not the mind. That's why merely repeating a salvation formula does not assure one is converted. Campers often learn more from the attitudes of leaders than from the lessons they teach. Quiet, informal, cabin devotions can be the moment of spiritual perception for many.

Another strange notion is the secular-sacred viewpoint, which suggests that camp offers *spiritual* things and other things. Bible class, prayer meetings, chapel, missionary hour, are "spiritual." All else is "other things," with negligible worth. How foolish! For the Chrisitan, Christ pervades all of life all of the time. Every relationship, each tear, every burst of laughter, all mystery, adventure, play, or luxurious loafing must partake of the quality called *spiritual*. God's Spirit does not hide in chapel awaiting the camper's arrival. God is just as interested in the overnight hike as He is in the missionary moment. How many missionaries have heard God's call on the wilderness trail! How many have discovered God's greatness in a thunderstorm. How many have sensed Christ's love through a helping hand up a steep place. Campers should be taught the "everywhereness" of God.

Yet campers need to be taught a disciplined devotional life. While all of life is truly spiritual, not all is *devotional*, and devotions are vital. The cabin group provides an excellent setting for teaching a meaningful devotional life.

We are all familiar with the campfire ceremony. "I promised the Lord last year at camp . . . but I failed." Most often the lack of personal devotions accounts for spiritual failure for both campers and leaders. Until a Christian cultivates a personal life with God, he must subsist on another's gospel. Regular personal Bible reading and prayer render the Christian self-sustaining before the Lord. Sharpen the tool of devotions.

GOD'S SOVEREIGN PURPOSE

The ultimate instrument for changing campers is the work of the Holy Spirit. Nothing else counts. If God's work is to be done, God must do it, though we are His tools.

This does not preclude our diligence and creativity, but unless we recognize Divine sovereignty, we're doomed to frustration. We do not always win. A camp that demands growing statistics is in jeopardy. Decisions induced by any means other than the work of the Holy Spirit are hollow at best.

As we faithfully teach the Scriptures and invite campers to Christ, responses can be expected. When Christians pray, God works. Though we cannot command God's sovereign purpose, He has invited us to become tools in His workmanship.

Somehow, what we are and do blends with God's purpose. This is an unspeakable, sublime mystery, and the strength for the camp counselor.

OBJECTIVES OF CHRISTIAN CAMPING

We have looked at the fundamental element in Christian camping: the impact of a dedicated, prepared counselor on the life of a young person. We have considered basic foundations and tools for camp counseling. One more factor must be addressed: the goal of Christian camping.

That goal is quite simple—to win campers to Christ and train them in God's ways through Bible study and Christian example.

Christians may serve in many worthy kinds of camping, all of them possessing Christian overtones. There are music camps, sports camps, fine arts camps, even computer camps. Spiritual values may emerge from any close relationship between Christian leaders and youngsters. But the goal of such camps is to produce musicians, athletes, artists, or proficient computer operators. A Christian camp, in our frame of reference, is one that seeks to produce growing Christians.

Evangelism and Bible teaching are essential to Christian camping, though these may be approached through many kinds of program activity. Evangelism and Bible discovery do not occur in some sort of religious vacuum. *Program* is the vehicle that carries camper and staff through the week in a challenging, worthy environment. Program can include almost anything, including music, sports, the fine arts, or computers! Bible study and worship will be prominent on the schedule. What makes a camp *Christian* is the determination to confront each camper with the claims of Christ on the individual.

Camps and other Christian institutions must always be on guard against the danger of program overwhelming purpose. Leaders easily focus on the skills they teach rather than the hearts of the campers. While excellence in program surely belongs in Christian camping, we must always keep foremost the skills of the spirit.

The pages that follow will discuss the counselor and the program. We will note that the staff works as a team to apply the program to the camper, and the camper to the program. We will see that *program* is the total camp experience, with every moment possessing spiritual potential.

We will discover that the Holy Spirit works in real-life settings, as well as in the chapel or around the campfire, putting down that dreadful dichotomy that views life in two separate compartments—the spiritual and unspiritual.

Camp requires many kinds of activity of the counselor, but your goal must always be clear: to win campers to Christ, and to model the gospel before them.

A Personal Note

Let me tell you why I believe so completely in Christian camping. It began many years ago on an historic campground in Minnesota. Red Rock Camp Meeting had continued for nearly a century when I got there at the age of thirteen. The camp boasted no lake or swimming pool. The recreation program was an occasional choose-up-sides ball game. Those so inclined could play with rusty horseshoes; real ones once worn by horses! Our cabin was an old frame house with running water only when it rained. Adults, children, youth, and the aged mingled freely.

Meetings were held several times daily in an open tabernacle with a bark-strewn, dirt floor. I recall the spirited singing, the shouting-Methodist preaching, the overpowering praying, and that long walk forward to a crude plank altar where I found new life in Christ. At Red Rock, I met Rev. Ed Rieff, the camp leader who changed my life through a providential phone call six years later.

A boy kneeling at an altar, and a man caring enough to befriend the boy, and living so God could nudge him to make a phone call at the moment of need. That's Christian camping and camp counseling.

Many settings can serve equally well for carrying out the objectives of Christian camping. I have ridden and hiked many mountain trails, canoed hundreds of wilderness miles, and preached in tabernacle pulpits. I have shivered in subzero Alaska camps. The setting is not the thing. The purpose and the people, they are everything.

Well, out there are eight or ten kids. They're wondering about you. What they become depends very much on what you are willing to become. Who knows what secrets God's Spirit may whisper to you? That's the trail that leads to camp.

2

Camping Backgrounds

This chapter will review the history and structure of Christian camping as background for understanding your role as a counselor. Camping has its philosophers, who sometimes argue with some heat their varying viewpoints. Your concern is to learn how *your* camp operates, and what it expects of the counselor.

We will note that Christian camping is not quite 200 years old, a product of the unique history of the U.S. and Canada. Contemporary Christian camping—with a major emphasis on youth—reaches back perhaps 50 years. Lacking a standard model or central authority, you would expect broad differences among camps. I have observed that success in camping relies far more on the quality and dedication of the staff than on a particular philosophy, structure, or program.

Most camps will provide prospective counselors with a staff manual. This becomes your primary guide, setting forth the organization and leadership pattern under which you will serve. Job titles and descriptions will vary from camp to camp, but certain, essential functions must be fulfilled in any group living situation. You will find yourself at the heart of your camping ministry. Many camp leaders feel you—the counselor—are *the* heart.

THE HISTORY OF CAMPING

The roots of Christian camping are entwined with the roots of other Christian institutions. A careful study of the history of

25

the Christian camping movement apparently has never been seriously undertaken. Perhaps the most thorough discussion is found in *An Introduction to Christian Camping* (Graendorf and Mattson, Eds., Moody Press, 1979) in the chapter on camping history by Dr. Clifford V. Anderson.

Anderson traces camping to the Greeks and Egyptians, who used camping for education and recreation. Christian camping began with the frontier camp meeting, as we shall note, before American educational and recreational camps began.

Camp Counseling, by Mitchell, Robberson, and Obley (an important book for every serious student of camping) provides a sketch of camping in the general field. This book credits William Gunn with founding the first camp in 1861, when Mr. Gunn exploited his pupils' enthusiasm for outdoor living in a variety of educational camping activities through 1879.

In 1876 Dr. Joseph Trimble Rothrock, a physician, experimented with a private health camp, but the experiment failed for lack of revenue. According to **Camp Counseling,** the first recorded church camp was launched by the Reverand George W. Hinkley in 1880, when he took seven boys on a camping trip to Gardner's Island near Wakefield, Rhode Island. The Reverend Hinkley later founded the Good Will Farm for Boys and offered a program not unlike that found in many Bible camps today.

The camp with the longest continuous history was founded in 1885 by Sumner F. Dudley, who later became a YMCA staff member. He continued camping with boys until his death at forty-three in 1897. The camp he was then associated with at Lake Champlain, Westport, New York, was named in his honor.

Yet in my opinion none of these camping pioneers deserves the title, "Grandfather of Christian Camping." That honor goes to some unknown Presbyterian clergyman who proposed to his brethren that a devotional exercise be conducted in northern Kentucky.

CANE RIDGE CAMP MEETING

Somewhere between 1800 and 1801, in the upper part of

Kentucky at a memorable place called "Cane Ridge," there was appointed a sacramental meeting by some of the Presbyterian ministers. At the meeting, seemingly unexpected by ministers or people, the mighty power of God was displayed in an extraordinary manner; many were moved to tears and bitter and loud crying for mercy. The meeting was kept up by night and day. Thousands heard of the mighty work, and came on foot, on horseback, in carriages and wagons. It was supposed that there were in attendance at times during the meeting from twelve to twenty-five thousand people. Hundreds fell prostrate under the mighty power of God, as men slain in battle. Stands were erected in the woods from which preachers of different churches proclaimed repentance toward God and faith in our Lord Jesus Christ, and it was supposed, by eye and ear witnesses, that between one and two thousand souls were happily and powerfully converted to God during the meeting. It was not unusual for one, two, three, and four to seven preachers to be addressing the listening thousands at the same time from the different stands erected for the purpose. The heavenly fire spread in almost every direction. It was said, by truthful witnesses, that at times more than one thousand persons broke out into loud shouting all at once, and that the shouts could be heard for miles around.

From this camp-meeting, for so it ought to be called, the news spread through all the Churches, and through all the land, and it excited great wonder and surprise; but it kindled a religious flame that spread all over Kentucky and through many other states. And I may here be permitted to say, that this was the first camp-meeting ever held in the United States, and here our camp-meetings took their rise.*

Now that was a camp! No history of Christian camping dares overlook the impact of the frontier camp meeting on the history of America or on the development of the camping movement. Eagle-eyed mothers tried, not always successfully, to keep ardent young swains a respectful distance from the maidens. Grandmothers sought to impress on junior boys the

*The Autobiography of Peter Cartwright (New York: Abingdon), 1956, pp. 33-34. Used by permission.

virtues of all-day preaching, also with limited success. Apparently no one had yet considered the potential of camp counselors.

But with the settling of the frontier and the sophistication of society, camp meetings passed from the raw, emotional spontaneity of Cane Ridge to orderly preaching and prayer conferences. Some survived to become the forerunners of today's Bible conference.

Somewhere along the line the needs of young people came into focus, and special features for youth were added to Bible conference programs. These in turn developed into youth camps which eclipsed for a time the parent conferences. But the past decade has witnessed the return of all-family camping in various forms, including the oldfashioned Bible conference.

The camping idea—Christians gathering outdoors for extended periods with spiritual objectives—reaches back to the beginnings of America, anticipating other forms of group camping by sixty years. The influence of camping on the growth of the church and the expansion of the missionary movement can scarcely be overemphasized, and I believe camping's greatest days are yet to come!

CAMPING PHILOSOPHY

The *why, what,* and *how* of Christian camping make up the philosophy of a camp. Many camps have developed a carefully-written philosophy statement, though some fine camps operate by sheer instinct, satisfied to let philosophy rest in the hearts and heads of the leaders.

Early youth camps were usually extensions of parent Bible conferences, with the focus on several all-camp meetings per day. To the leaders of those camps, the chapel was central, and you find this reflected in the layout of the camp. The chapel was the dominant structure. Teaching/preaching specialists formed the core of the staff. Counselors served as little more than chaperones. Not much value was placed on activity that filled the hours between religious gatherings. While great good was accomplished in those camps, some leaders began to feel restless about this *centralized* philosophy, with its focus on all-camp programs.

This restlessness grew in part out of the success of education and agency camps that were flourishing. They functioned chiefly through small living units led by a trained counselor. The spiritual possibilities in such an arrangement were clear. It was so easy for a camper to get lost in the crowd in traditional, centralized camps. Slowly Christian youth camping moved toward the decentralized philosophy, though modifying it to retain the values of some all-camp gatherings.

The term *eclectic camping* was coined by the editors of *Introduction to Christian Camping* to describe the typical camp of today, a blend of centralized and decentralized thinking.

The transition was not without tension, and traces remain today. But as camp leaders recognized the potential of the counselor and the cabin group, eclectic camping gained favor. The preacher and teacher share with the counselor in working toward the camp's spiritual goals. Today we find an almost universal recognition of the essential role of the counselor.

CAMP ORGANIZATION

The struggle over camp philosphy was paralleled by an evolution within staffing and structure. Since the roots of Christian camping lay in the church, its organizers and prime movers were almost exclusively clergymen. Since the major purpose for holding camp was to gather as many as possible into the chapel for preaching, the tabernacle became the dominent building and influence. Almost no thought was given to the hours between meetings.

Of course meals were necessary, hence a dining hall and food service staff. Things did break and buildings needed care. A maintenance crew was added. But the thought of a recreation director or craft instructor was slow to emerge. Anyone who felt so inclined could lay out a ballfield or drive horseshoe stakes.

We noted earlier that counselors were viewed solely as

chaperones, charged with keeping reasonable order among the young. Children stayed with parents in all early camps. But as the Bible conference took form as an institution, the needs of youth came to be recognized, and the counselor's role evolved. Today most camp leaders affirm the key function of the counselor within the staff. As the family-centered, adult-oriented Bible conference faded and youth camping emerged, new organizational patterns were called for.

Organizational charts are much loved by camp boards and directors. Indeed, charts are useful tools—but not without potential dangers.

A typical chart places the sponsoring agency supreme, just above the camp board. Beneath the board, radiating in all directions, solid and dotted lines dash to and fro connecting directors, committees, assistant directors, and ultimately you. The chart visualizes lines of responsibility and authority, and if you look closely, you find the camper lying wistfully somewhere near the bottom of the page, connected to you.

Here lies the danger of the charts. Organization can loom so large in the minds of leaders that *purpose* is forgotten. *Camp is for the camper.* The objective for every leader is the spiritual good of each camper. It might be helpful to reverse the order in the charts, and place the camper on top.

CAMP LEADERSHIP

Today's Christian camps operate under team leadership. Jobs and job descriptions vary from camp to camp, but the nature of camping demands certain kinds of people. Your camp manual will no doubt identify staff roles and relationships. It is essential that the counselor understand where he or she fits the organization plan. Whatever other assignments may fall to you, your primary concern will be the campers who share life with you in your cabin.

A careful, continuing study of Romans 12 will equip you well for serving on the camp team. Read this chapter several times a day through the weeks preceding camp. *Living Letters* offers a particularly refreshing interpretation of Romans 12:6a: "God has given each of us the ability to do certain things well." This is a good word for you as a counselor, suggesting that God has given you special gifts, and that others also have particular gifts. Don't attempt to do everyone's work!

Interfering with other staff members only creates tension. Unless the safety of a camper is at stake, avoid involvement in other cabin groups. You may indeed beam a stern eye at a chapel offender, or gently redirect energies that threaten peace in the canteen-line, but respect the leadership responsibilities of each staff member.

Pause extra long at Romans 12:18. *Living Letters* again paraphrases the text aptly. "Don't quarrel with anyone. Be at peace with everyone, just as much as you possibly can." Ill feelings between leaders are quickly felt by campers, so extend your ministry to fellow workers as well as campers. Since all leaders are quite human, they experience low moments. Absorbing a staff member's temporary irritation will enrich everyone. A quarrel has seldom arisen that would not end immediately if one party simply ceased talking!

Respect the chain of command. Sometimes you will be tempted to flee to the camp director with a matter that should be taken to your head counselor. Or you may feel like scolding the maintenance man. Above all, resist the urge to complain about the state of the oatmeal. The cook already knows, and the anguish in the kitchen exceeds yours.

Unpleasant assignments may fall to you. Do them quickly and without complaint, even though others seem to escape such duty. Romans 12 speaks of a "living sacrifice." A sacrifice is beyond complaining. The sight of a counselor polishing a toilet bowl with a brush, a smile, and a song will speak to the heart of a camper. That might be the mystic moment of discovery, who can tell?

For the most part your role as counselor includes responsibility for a small number of campers who live in your cabin. You may be assigned a program responsibility as well. In some camps, the counselor is asked to take on another duty—the supervision of a junior counselor or a counselor-in-training.

THE COUNSELOR AND THE CIT

The development of new leaders is one of Christian camping's major contributions to the church. Many camps pursue an aggressive program to grow their own leaders. While this places an added responsibility on you, accept the task cheerfully.

Be prepared to give willing leadership when a CIT is assigned to you. Many successful CIT programs place trainees in housing apart from campers, with visits to cabins for specific training purposes. Some camps place trainees in the cabin as an assistant counselor. Beware of making a trainee half camper and half leader, a situation with potential problems.

A poor approach finds a counselor assigning the more unpleasant tasks to the trainee, or overloading him or her with duties. The proper approach finds the counselor and trainee sharing leadership under the counselor's thoughtful guidance.

A real problem results when a trainee polarizes the cabin group, sometimes negating the counselor's efforts. If this situation is discovered, the counselor should take immediate corrective steps through proper channels. A CIT must never be allowed to interfere with the spiritual well-being of campers.

A well-structured, properly supervised CIT program belongs in camping as a natural extension of the camp's spiritual ministry. The cabin counselor becomes part of the teaching team, guiding future staffers into the joys of leadership.

THE COUNSELOR: A TEAM MEMBER

Since staff titles and roles will vary, you are referred to your camp manual for details of the leadership team on which you will serve. Certain counselor staff relationships will be discussed in the chapters that follow as specific topics are reviewed. You will be assisted by the camp nurse, lead counselor, program director, camp pastor, etc. I would stress again the importance of learning your role and working within it, carefully avoiding trespass on the duties of others.

Probably regular opportunity will be provided during the camp week for your personal growth and relaxation. The one-week counselor may not feel so keenly the need for support and rest, but share enthusiastically in any respite from duty your camp provides! By the close of the week you'll know why.

Staff meetings for evaluation, training, and prayer are valuable means for personal growth. Sharing concerns and successes distributes the burdens and blessings of your cabin through the entire staff. Aggressive participation in staff meetings is one of the counselor's assignments.

While Proverbs 11:14 probably refers to circumstances other than camp, it seems appropriate here. "In the multitude of counselors there is safety." Many a rebel camper has been tamed through a staff prayer meeting.

Christian leaders often suffer the danger of self-neglect in the busyness of serving others. Cultivate an attitude of prayer. Discipline your day to include personal devotions, perhaps in company with your campers. The counselor who maintains a quiet, constant dialogue with his own spirit concerning matters of faith and godliness finds a source of strength unknown by those who become overwhelmed by leadership burdens.

THE COUNSELOR AND THE CAMPER

An understanding of staff relationships and program assignments is vital to your job, but I would call you back again to the central purpose that brings you to camp: your campers. The next chapter will lead you into a detailed study of their makeup and needs, and your responsibilities as the cabin-group leader. The values of Christian camping overflow to enrich many: the staff, the family, the churches, the campers' homes, but your assignment remains that handful of boys or girls who share life with you for a week or more. Camp is for the camper.

3

The Cabin Group

ONE OF THE MORE UNNERVING MOMENTS in my brief career as a substitute teacher occurred in a Michigan elementary school. The principal handed me the day's assignment with unusual solicitude. I was to teach *kindergarten!* That proved to be the longest day in my life as a teacher, one I never allowed to happen again.

My problem was neither a lack of concern nor sincerity. I just didn't understand little kids. You can expect trials of like magnitude if you fail to acquaint yourself with the characteristics of your campers. Every group will contain one or more youngsters laden with exceptions. Sometimes you may think *none* of your campers is normal, but ordinarily you will succeed in meeting day-by-day challenges if you learn to know your campers.

KNOWING YOUR CAMPERS

The developmental characteristics that follow are reprinted from *These Are Your Children* by Jenkins, Schacter, and Bauer.* The authors give the following advice:

> Children are not small adults. They do not think, feel, or react as adults. They do not have the knowledge, judgment, or background to choose experiences that will be beneficial to them and to reject those that may be harm-

*Reprinted by permission of the publisher, Scott, Foresman, Glenview, IL.

35

ful. At the same time we cannot judge or measure them by adult standards. Children need grown-ups who can thoughtfully lead the way through the confusion of our times. The first responsibility of those who sincerely want to help children to grow up ready to take their part in this changing world is to try to understand the world of children; the general pattern according to which all children grow and, within this framework, the individual needs and characteristics of each particular child for whom they are responsible.

About Eight

PHYSICAL DEVELOPMENT

Growth still slow and steady—arms lengthening, hands growing.
Eyes ready for both near and far vision.
    Near-sightedness may develop this year.
Permanent teeth continuing to appear.
Large muscles still developing. Small muscles better developed, too. Manipulative skills are increasing.
Attention span getting longer.
Poor posture may develop.

CHARACTERISTIC BEHAVIOR

Often careless, noisy, argumentative, but also alert, friendly, interested in people.
More dependent on his mother, less so on his teacher.
    Sensitive to criticism.
New awareness of individual differences.
Eager, more enthusiastic than cautious. Higher accident rate.
Gangs beginning. Best friends of same sex.
Allegiance to other children instead of to an adult in case of conflict.
Greater capacity for self-evaluation.
Much spontaneous dramatization, ready for simple classroom dramatics.
Understanding of time and use of money.

Responsive to group activities, both spontaneous and adult-supervised.

Fond of team games, comics, television, movies, adventure stories, collections.

SPECIAL NEEDS

Praise and encouragement from adults.

Reminders of his responsibilities.

Wise guidance and channeling of his interests and enthusiasms, rather than domination or unreasonable standards.

A best friend.

Experience of belonging to peer group—opportunity to identify with others of same age and sex.

Adult-supervised groups and planned after-school activities.

Exercise of both large and small muscles.

ABOUT NINE OR TEN

PHYSICAL DEVELOPMENT

Slow, steady growth continues—girls forge further ahead. Some children reach the plateau preceding the preadolescent growth spurt.

Lungs as well as digestive and circulatory systems almost mature.

Heart especially subject to strain.

Teeth may need straightening. First and second bicuspids appearing.

Eye-hand coordination good. Ready for crafts and shop work.

Eyes almost adult size. Ready for close work with less strain.

CHARACTERISTIC BEHAVIOR

Decisive, responsible, dependable, reasonable, strong sense of right and wrong.

Individual differences distinct, abilities now apparent.

Capable of prolonged interest. Often makes plans and goes ahead on his own.

Gangs strong, or short duration and changing membership. Limited to one sex.

Perfectionist—wants to do well, but loses interest if discouraged or pressured.

Interested less in fairy tales and fantasy, more in his community and country and in other countries and peoples.

Loyal to his country and proud of it.

Spends a great deal of time in talk and discussion. Often outspoken and critical of adults, although still dependent on adult approval.

Frequently argues over fairness in games.

Wide discrepancies in reading ability.

SPECIAL NEEDS

Active rough and tumble play.

Friends and membership in a group.

Training in skills, but without pressure.

Books of many kinds, depending on individual reading level and interest.

Reasonable explanations without talking down.

Definite responsibility.

Frank answers to his questions about coming physiological changes.

THE PREADOLESCENT

PHYSICAL DEVELOPMENT

A "resting period," followed by a period of rapid growth in height and then growth in weight. This usually starts sometime between 9 and 13. Boys may mature as much as two years later than girls.

Girls usually taller and heavier than boys.

Reproductive organs maturing. Secondary sex characteristics developing.

Rapid muscular growth.

Uneven growth of different parts of the body.

Enormous but often capricious appetite.

CHARACTERISTIC BEHAVIOR

Wild range of individual differences in maturity level.

Gangs continue, though loyalty to the gang stronger in boys than in girls.

Interest in team games, pets, television, radio, movies, comics. Marked interest differences between boys and girls.

Teasing and seeming antagonism between boys' and girls' groups.

Awkwardness, restlessness, and laziness common as result of rapid and uneven growth.

Opinion of own group beginning to be valued more highly than that of adults.

Often becomes overcritical, changeable, rebellious, uncooperative.

Self-conscious about physical changes.

Interest in earning money.

SPECIAL NEEDS

Understanding of the physical and emotional changes about to come.

Skillfully planned school and recreation programs to meet needs of those who are approaching puberty as well as those who are not.

Opportunities for greater independence and for carrying more responsibility without pressure.

Warm affection and sense of humor in adults. No nagging, condemnation, or talking down.

Sense of belonging, acceptance by peer group.

THE ADOLESCENT

PHYSICAL DEVELOPMENT

Rapid weight gain at beginning of adolescence. Enormous appetite.

Sexual maturity, with accompanying physical and emotional changes. Girls are usually about two years ahead of boys.

Sometimes a period of glandular imbalance.

Skeletal growth completed, adult height reached, musuclar coordination improved.

Heart growing rapidly at beginning of period.

CHARACTERISTIC BEHAVIOR

Going to extremes, emotional instability with "knowing-it-all" attitude.

Return of habits of younger child—nail biting, tricks, impudence, day-dreaming.

High interest in philosophical, ethical, and religious problems. Search for ideals.

Preoccupation with acceptance by the social group. Fear of ridicule and of being unpopular. Oversensitiveness and self-pity.

Strong identification with an admired adult.

Assertion of independence from family as a step toward adulthood.

Responds well to group responsibility and group participation. Groups may form cliques.

High interest in physical attractiveness.

Girls usually more interested in boys than boys in girls, resulting from earlier maturing of the girls.

SPECIAL NEEDS

Acceptance by and conformity with others of own age.

Adequate understanding of sexual relationships and attitudes.

Kind, unobtrusive, adult guidance which does not threaten the adolescent's feelings of freedom.

Assurance of security. Adolescents seek both dependence and independence.

Opportunities to make decisions and to earn and save money.

Provision for constructive recreation. Some cause, idea, or issue to work for.

These lists summarize general characteristics which will suggest behavioral responses typical of the age-groupings commonly found in camp. You should understand that this is only a general guide. Many campers will exhibit some degree of variance. Unfortunately, you cannot rely on campers to mature at the same rate. There must be a careful appraisal of each individual. But if you know how a *typical* junior, junior high, or high school camper can be expected to respond, you can lead with confidence.

Obviously your approach to leadership must be adjusted to the capabilities of your group. A first-year camper must be treated gently. This may be his first extended stay away from home and mother. A high school senior requires nearly adult treatment. He will be offended by any suggestion of juvenile condescension.

I cannot stress too much the importance of this matter. Expecting too much or too little from campers is a primary source of counselor failures.

Knowing Each Camper

A knowledge of general camper characteristics should be followed by a continuing effort to discover the nature and needs of each camper. The lower the camper-counselor ratio, the greater the potential for effective work. Begin by mastering each camper's name. A name tag will prove helpful for the first day. You may wish to offer some honor to the camper who first identifies every cabinmate by name. Use the camper's name each time you speak to him or her. Post a cabin roster, identifying campers by bed location.

Bear in mind that campers are discovering your characteristics at the same time you are learning theirs! The age-old struggle between youth and authority sets in immediately, as well as the inevitable tussle for sovereignity within the peer group. Your campers will probably know you before you know them. The first hour will go far toward establishing your leadership.

Campers will type you as friendly, approachable, fun-loving; stiff, authoritarian, or aloof. First impressions are hard to change. If you sincerely love your campers and enjoy being with them, most will respond with friendship. But don't think that love demands overfamiliarity. Be slow to allow campers first-name privileges, though local tradition may alter this.

Most campers will be anxious to please you, though a few will go to great lengths to hide the fact. A few campers may resist leadership, and you cannot force your way into their friendship. A camper's first response often reveals basic spiritual needs. Sloppy Sue's bunk is a mess. Apple-polishing Anne dogs your steps. Shy Sharon needs your attention, though she hides from you. Grumpy Girtie pouts on her lower bunk, coveting the more favorable altitude of Sneaky Sal's upper bunk. Sneaky Sal has hidden a contraband radio in the niche where roof meets wall. The characteristics of individual campers begin to emerge as the cabin group takes shape. Here is your challenge for the week.

You must resist the temptation to classify campers into "I-like" and "I-don't-like" groups. And you will never engage in petty contests of will with children, contests you can never win. Unlovely campers present the greatest challenge.

You will learn to judge which campers require more personal attention, and what kind of attention. Use wisdom in pairing off campers as bunkmates. Some camps separate close friends and campers from a common church as a policy, but this should be done carefully. The only security some campers know is an established friend.

As soon as possible, begin to learn your campers' backgrounds. Some camps provide a camper profile for counselors. Casual conversation and careful listening will reveal much about an individual.

I recall a junior boy named Fred who pegged himself as the bad-news camper by turning the first meal into chaos. Fred's manners were unspeakable. He continually annoyed those seated near him, and he brought down the wrath of his counselor. No one told the counselor that this lad had no dad, and his mother entertained a variety of men in the home. Trouble was the norm for this troubled boy, so why change at camp? Fred's kind are relatively few, but understanding his background could have helped the counselor minister with greater patience.

Organizing the Cabin Group

Each camp builds traditions that determine the kind of system you will develop for life in your cabin. Standards for dress, conduct, and conversation may differ from those practiced in a camper's home. Since a measure of regimentation is necessary, guidelines should be clearly explained.

In spite of much grumbling about rules, campers appreciate such guidelines. You may doctor up rules by calling them traditions, which is fine; but whatever the name, make sure campers understand. Encourage discussion. Someone will probably ask about the penalty for breaking rules. The discipline pattern and your determination to enforce rules should be understood.

There will often be gray areas. Magazines and books of doubtful value should be discouraged. Radios and tape recorders are generally banned to preserve a wholesome tone. The spiritual need of young people caught up in the smoking habit calls for thoughtful consideration. To me it is quite unthinkable that a counselor would indulge this harmful habit. Be alert for the presence of drugs. The prevalence of marijuana and other narcotics among young people makes it inevitable that camps must deal with the problem.

Equally deadly and as common as drugs is the infiltration of pornography. Neither problem calls for a response of rage or shock. Addicts of drugs and pornography desperately need Christ. You can expect both problems to crop up in camp, especially among older groups. A strategy should be determined to help the campers.

Older campers may drive cars or motorcycles to camp. Ordinarily keys are turned in at the time of registration. Counselors should learn staff vehicle regulations also.

Occasionally you will find a camper who needs counsel concerning dress standards, on and off the beach. Generally a kind, firm word will remove the problem. In co-ed camps restricted areas should be clearly defined and wholesome boy-girl relationships expected. Dating traditions vary in camps. Overt, immature displays of affection should be discouraged. Counselors sometimes need reminders too! When campers need help, understanding, straight-forward counsel should be given.

An objective, discussion of standards for a wholesome, spiritually enriching atmosphere usually serves better than a detailed list of rules. Where specific boundaries are needed, they should be clearly presented. Let campers know what is expected. But what can you do with borderline issue? Some matters do not lend themselves to legislation. What are *short* shorts? Or when is a modest two-piece swim suit to be preferred over immodest one-piece attire? Which books and magazines are suitable? What music is acceptable?

Such issues provide grist for the counselor's mill. A candid exploring of issues opens both counselor and campers to mutual understanding. Don't expect easy answers, but look for stimulating, creative discussion to help campers discover truth.

The maximum camp penalty is of course expulsion. Campers should know this possibility exists. The counselor's responsibility for discipline should be kept at a minimum. Discipline will be discussed in greater detail later in the chapter.

THE DAILY SCHEDULE

Posting a full schedule cannot assure a happy week for your campers. The schedule is but a skeleton on which you must hang muscle and meat. Younger campers especially need encouragement to become involved in camp activities. To a large measure, you determine the program. The role of the counselor is to relate the camper to the total camp program. Campers will often overlook activities you ignore.

Most camps expect counselors to spend a major portion of the day with their cabin groups. Perhaps you will be asked to plan the day's program for your cabin group. If so, include your campers in the planning. Aim at variety with the campers' needs and interests in mind.

Seek maximum involvement for every camper, and work hardest in behalf of a reticent group member. Though a program specialist may be in charge, your presence will encourage campers. Friendships built during crafts and play create the climate you need to touch a camper's heart during devotions. Often, in the mysterious manner of God's working, a camper's moment of discovery may come at a non-devotional time.

Bear in mind that effective counseling does not require mastery of every sport or craft. You may be a learner along with your campers, and sometimes you must bow to their superior skill! Nothing pleases a camper more than helping his counselor tie a proper knot or correct an irregular braid.

However you organize the day, spend as much time as possible with your campers, thrusting them deeply into the camp program. You may be expected to attend a staff meeting while your campers are under the care of another leader. Or you may be granted a blessed hour for relaxation away from your campers. Take it! But covet every opportunity to be with your cabin group.

Many camps have adopted the good practice of assigning counselors a Bible teaching role. This demands added preparation, but the spiritual potential makes it worthwhile. Other camps secure Bible teaching specialists, just as sports and craft specialists are engaged. Whatever pattern your camp follows, you will find your presence in class and chapel most helpful.

The attention span of campers is discouragingly brief, and the setting for class or worship often includes built-in distractions. Once, high in the Montana Rockies, I witnessed the frustration of a camp pastor who had launched into an extended pre-breakfast sermonette. A log semicircle was inhabited by sixty hungry, wiggling juniors, while the minister unlimbered his three-pointer. Then two red squirrels launched a game of tag in the pines immediately over his head. The few who hadn't noticed the squirrels did so when the pastor commanded the campers, "Stop watching those animals and *pay attention!*"

I'm not convinced it was the devil who sent those squirrels, as was intimated. The event precipitated worthwhile conversation during rest-hour devotions that afternoon, and later on in an informal staff meeting.

The presence of counselors helps campers gain maximum value from chapel and Bible class under the best or worst conditions. The counselor also gains valuable points of contact for cabin devotions. Camps often fail to minister as effectively as they might, simply because of the quantity of unrelated data poured out daily before the camper. Only the truth *perceived* provides lasting value. When you build cabin devotions upon the ideas presented in class or chapel, you strengthen the probability for spiritual perception.

Don't hesitate to sit with campers bent on amusing or annoying one another in chapel. Usually this gesture restores order. Older campers require a bit more subtle treatment. A row of counselors seated in the rear of the chapel has little value.

If you would make camp a memorable experience for your cabin group, plan to involve them in as much of the program as possible. Enter into activities with them, paying special heed to the reluctant camper. Share as many of their daily experiences as possible. Be among them in Bible study and worship. Watch for spiritual responses, and keep alert for thoughts you can use in cabin devotions.

LIGHTS OUT!

Camp becomes a total experience for most campers, each part enriching the day: the ball field, the beach, the dining hall, the chapel. Every staff member adds his or her personal contribution to the store of treasures a camper will carry home. The adventure of cabin life rates high in its memory-building potential.

One-by-one your campers gather inside, and the door is finally closed for the night. Then your skill as a counselor is tested, and few tests can compare with the first night!

Even veteran counselors approach the first night in camp with trepidation. Counselors are made of less stern stuff than campers, and welcome the tolling of the lights-out bell. But campers feel otherwise. When you think about it, a bell has little to do with sleep. Campers sleep only when they are sleepy.

Consider the nonsleep factors found that first night at camp.

Nothing is like home, where campers live 51 weeks of the year. The group may be composed of people who barely know each other. The struggle to find a place in the peer-group hierarchy has set in. The beds are strange and perhaps uncomfortable. A day of travel and exciting experiences lie behind each camper. And there is the counselor whom tradition dictates campers must test! How futile to intone, "Lights out. Everyone go to sleep."

Turning lights out is comparatively easy (except for flashlights). Inducing sleep is exceedingly difficult. Every camper turns into a ventriloquist, with an amazing repertoire of weird sounds. A spirit hurls a tennis shoe through the darkness. An errant frog may have found its way into the counselor's bed. You are no match for a cabin full of juniors, much less a cabin full of high schoolers. You can't lick them, so join them! Make the first night fun.

I have on occasion met an authoritarian person who declares that *he* tolerates no nonsense from campers the first night in camp. When he says quiet, he means *quiet*. Then I observe him at an adult retreat. He asserts his adult prerogative to ignore the printed schedule, which establishes the hour for lights-out and quiet. Extended political or theological debates flow endlessly on the premise that adults sleep when they grow sleepy. Youthful campers will do likewise.

The secret to success the first night in camp is to help your campers become sleepy. Sensible bedtime hours are vital for health, and equally vital is sensible planning to bring weariness to an optimum level at approximately the same time as the lights-out bell. This requires nothing short of genius.

Agree to limit noise levels to the confines of the cabin. Campers will ordinarily understand the need for this, particularly when they feel that too much noise will bring down the wrath of the head counselor on their cabin counselor. You might suggest that possibility. You might also suggest, for safety sake, that all campers remain in bed after the lights are out. Be aware of security needs should it be necessary for campers to make a midnight trip to the washroom.

Extended devotions have a marvelous capacity to induce

drowsiness. You may abbreviate them later, but on the first night take full advantage of this resource. You will *not* say, "All you good Christians will go right to sleep." Some of our finest church leaders were holy terrors in camp, particularly the first night. Never threaten what you can't perform. Declaring, "The very next camper who makes a noise will be sent straight home," is an irresistible challenge.

The finest device I know to maintain cabin serenity is a story, a long one, your very best story. It may or may not possess a religious lesson. It must not be designed to terrify campers, or even mildly scare them. Perhaps the ghost story has a place in camp, but the first night is surely not that place! If you can introduce a continued story to run all week, happy are you.

There is no surefire formula for gracefully putting campers to sleep the first night. Make them as tired as possible. Involve them in happy group sharing at bedtime. Then focus their energies through a story until sleep comes. Then you can sleep too.

"DAYLIGHT IN THE SWAMP!"

This historic cry from the lumber camp has been replaced by the camp bell, which rings distressingly early. However, a problem often overlooked by beginning counselors is the early riser, a camper who may anticipate the rising bell by hours. He tends to forget that most of the camp is still sleeping. Explain that all campers are to remain in bed until the rising signal.

Campers rarely need encouragement to get up the first morning, but on succeeding days you must help some. Early rising is a chief contributor to a quiet cabin at lights out, but beware of the camper who naps all afternoon!

Your camp tradition will determine the morning sequence of activities. Flag-rising usually precedes breakfast. Cabin cleanup often follows. Younger campers require assistance to keep personal gear and the cabin in good order. A daily inspection with honor accorded the cleanest cabin helps motivate campers. One camp created the Clean Clem award for the best cabin, the Dirty Gertie award for the poorest. This was appreciated by everyone, except the Gertrudes and Clemens who happened to attend camp.

Juniors often need reminders about grooming. Some boys will return home in the clothes they wore to camp if you are not alert. Counselors of girls will find good use for a spare hairbrush. Inspect younger campers for personal cleanliness. Mention the purpose of soap, water, and toothbrush. Of course, no camper is permitted to sleep in his clothes, but do not be surprised if a camper refuses to undress. Allow him the dignity of putting on his pajamas after lights-out.

When counseling young campers, check all beds in an inconspicuous manner. Emotional stresses and unrestricted access to canteen beverages may result in wet beds, even among campers not normally troubled. Again, guard the dignity of the camper as much as possible. Wet bedding and night clothing must be washed. Chronic bed-wetters should be supplied a moisture-proof mattress cover.

Between the rising bell and lights-out you will be responsible for several cabin activities. Cultivate good cabin etiquette to provide a happy mood. It's hard to enjoy any part of camp if a cabinmate left a muddy footprint in the middle of your cot. Each camper's bunk is his castle, though younger campers may need occasional reminders to tidy their castles.

Since cabins tend to become overcrowded, only personal effects should be stored inside. Athletic gear, clotheslines, hiking sticks, and all livestock belong outdoors. Livestock includes mice, frogs, turtles, lizards, tadpoles, and snakes. Be sure the clothesline is safely located away from travel routes, and well above the head level. A low-hanging line can be lethal to a camper dashing through the darkness.

Accidents in and around the cabin usually result from carelessness or horseplay. Teach respect for camp property. Rafters are not for climbing, and beds should never be walked on; truths young campers may not have discovered. While these matters may appear obvious, the counselor's presence remains the best antidote for cabin mischief that could result in damage or injury.

CABIN DEVOTIONS

Cabin devotions can be the most meaningful part of camp life, or they can be miserable exercises in endurance. Your camp may supply devotional guides correlated with other teaching and worship content. I wish more camps would adopt this practice. But often you will be expected to prepare your own cabin devotions.

The three basic ingredients for good cabin devotions are Scripture, prayer, and sharing. The lecture simply has no place. Select a brief Bible portion, preferably correlated with the chapel service or Bible study class. Remember, there is a difference in purpose between Bible class and devotions. Avoid using cabin devotions as a time for reviewing memory verses. Attention lags when several campers struggle through half-memorized passages. You might, however, select a memory verse as the Scripture for cabin devotions and quote it in unison with your campers.

Devotion time should be camper centered. Prayer concerns may be shared, then assigned to individuals. You may devise a method for establishing prayer partners within the group. Try "prayer chips," writing each camper's name on a chip of wood and allowing campers to draw partners. Praying around the circle should be practiced only when you are certain all campers are comfortable praying aloud. Introduce conversational prayer, and don't hestitate to remind campers that long-winded prayers are best practiced in private.

Sharing is the key to effective group devotions. Without participation, the exercise does not really become devotions. When the maturity level permits, encourage campers to share leadership. Let them read the Scripture. You may wish to divide into smaller groups for prayer. The word *discussion* frightens some people, so I prefer the word sharing. Any time a camper talks in the group, he is sharing, for better or worse. Really sharing is more than a glib testimony. To share means to take what is yours and give it to another. Encourage expression of familiar, simple things in nontheological language. And fight the urge to sermonize on each camper's contribution!

Equal in challenge to building group devotions is helping campers develop a meaningful, personal quiet time. The after-lunch rest hour offers the best hope for success. Your example will be the best motivation for campers. Suggest a simple pattern: Bible reading, meditation, and prayer. If the camp does not supply a quiet-time guide, allow your campers to help put one together.

Cabin Bible study and worship will be discussed in greater detail in a later chapter.

CABIN DUTY

Many camps have abandoned the work details which once formed a normal part of camp life, such as dining hall cleanup and dishwashing. Probably this is for the best. Cabin cleanup remains a significant daily chore, however, and we have already alluded to Clean Clem and Dirty Gertie.

Organize your group so that necessary work is shared equally. A duty roster posted in the cabin allows campers to plan their day, and also helps you know whom to look for when some work isn't done! Some of the pain of work is removed if you allow the campers to help draw up the duty roster. Create a sense of pride in your cabin appearance.

You may discover opportunities for service projects that can help build cabin pride. Beach cleanup, marking athletic fields, cleaning and marking nature trails, planting trees, building stone retaining walls; any useful work to improve or beautify the camp can build camper interest. Projects should not be too demanding, however, and always carefully supervised. Consult your camp director for instructions.

Your function as a counselor is to relate the camper to the total camp program. Avoid any activity not approved by the camp director which might create jealousy among other campers. Treating your campers to a secret party—which never remains a secret —is unfair to the counselor who may lack the money to treat his or her cabin. If your camp includes a cabin party night in the schedule, fine; but such a plan should be worked out and financed by the campers within prescribed limits.

Athletic competition between cabins may not always strengthen the overall camp spirit, since cabin groups seldom enjoy balance in strength or skill. A representative from each cabin may compete in an all-camp event, when the opportunity for winning is reasonably equal; a pie-eating contest, for example.

Cabin groups may be encouraged to go on hikes, cookouts, campouts or field trips. If you plan an outing, check each camper to make certain nothing is forgotten, and pace the activity to the capabilities of your group. Outings are for fun, not for hurting. Campouts and nature activity will be discussed in a later chapter.

Sooner or later, the time comes for stunt night. Monitor your campers' plans carefully to make sure their selection is in good taste, and not threatening to any cabinmate or camp leader. And make certain someone is coordinating the whole program. What could be more demoralizing than to discover Mohawk Cabin performing your skit before your turn comes?

Several sources for skits and stunts are listed in the bibliography, but if you can stir your campers' creative juices, they may think up something original or give a tired old skit a refreshing twist. Simple, brief skits come across more effectively than complex dramas. Use as many of your campers as possible.

CABIN CONTROL

The first camp I attended as a boy had a well-developed solution for the problem of restless campers. It was a Scout camp, and we were somewhat awed by the uniformed adult and youth leaders. When taps sounded, quiet reigned. Almost. A low murmur that ended soon brought no wrath. Even a snicker was tolerated. But persistent disturbance from one or more in a cabin meant swift judgment, usually for the whole cabin.

With no regard for justice, we were marched out onto the

gravel path for an exercise known as squad walking. We marched barefoot the length of the camp and back, a distance of several blocks, without a sound. Some patrols required several trips before utter silence was achieved. We knew this to be cruel and inhumane treatment, but I suppose, secretly, we felt honored by such attention. Seldom did a cabin require more than one treatment.

I don't recommend such discipline, though it proved effective. I do believe leadership should exercise authority and discipline chronic offenders. The best antidote to restlessness is tiredness. Keep your campers going full steam all day and close the evening with pleasant, quiet activity. And by all means deny the cabin noisemaker the luxury of an afternoon nap!

Often one or two campers create nighttime problems, and you may find it necessary to deal with them through disciplinary channels. If most campers find sleep difficult to gain, something is wrong with the schedule. The problem usually decreases as the week wears on. A rule demanding utter silence at the bell is both ill advised and unenforceable.

Discipline should not be viewed as an ugly word. In spite of the best programs and the finest plans, some campers will create disturbances. Often you will immediately spot potential trouble in a camper's attitude, but don't write off such a person. Bear in mind that troublesome campers most need the camp. Give your best effort to cultivating friendship with aggressive cabin members.

I visited an elderly couple in the home church of a dignified, austere denominational leader. "You should have known him when he was a camper," said the old man. "He was a holy terror!" This can be said of many Christian leaders. The same qualities that enable an adolescent to organize his cabin into a reign of terror for the counselor can later propel him into leadership. But remember that there's a difference between wholesome pranks and malicious conduct.

If the camp is properly organized, you will know the discipline limits within which you operate, and you can explain these limits to your campers. Those who persistently create trouble must be disciplined, and they should know in advance the action they can expect. Except for verbal sparring which never seems to end, avoid disciplining campers in the presence of others. This is probably what they want. A quiet, private talk is more effective.

Your responsibility seldom goes beyond this. Refer problem campers to the head counselor or to another staff member assigned to this task. Explain to the camper that rules require this. Except for deeply disturbed youngsters, the prospect of a confrontation with an adult away from the security of the peer group is frightening. Kinds and degrees of punishment should be worked out by the camp management and applied equally to all campers. Leniency in one cabin and severity in another damages the camp spirit.

Never allow behavior to become an emotional contest between you and a camper. You may win a grudging apology or conformity, but you haven't won the camper. There is no magic formula in disciplining. You can only meet problems as they arise. I don't really know why some adults can master a group of children, while others completely collapse. But if you lack the qualities to command a respectful hearing, you probably shouldn't be a counselor.

I discover my discipline problems run in inverse proportion to my degree of preparation. When I am enthusiastic and ready, most campers come along. Since I am not struggling with ill-prepared materials, I am at ease to handle an occasional attention lapse.

Prepare carefully for your ministry of leading your group. Campers who enjoy cabin life enter the total camp program with a receptive spirit, but trouble in the cabin casts a pall over the whole camp day.

4

All Together Now

While the counselor's duties discussed in Chapter 3 represent the most fruitful opportunities you will have for touching campers' lives for the Lord, the hours spent with other cabin groups are equally important for a spiritually effective camp. How much time will be given to all-camp activity depends on the philosophy that shapes the program of the camp you will serve.

Morning, Noon, And Night

Recently I vistied a camp serving 150 junior boys and girls. The program was excellent until we gathered for lunch, then the campers degenerated into barbarians, and the counselors weren't much better. There was raucous laughter, playing with food, reaching across the table, and frequent spills. I suggested to one leader that the noise level was intolerable. He yelled, "This is a camp!"

That was my point exactly. Since this was a Christian camp, I wondered why kids should be acting like hoodlums. Good manners surely belong within the pale of Chrisitan doctrine! The conduct I observed was boorish and inexcusable. Hopefully the camp you serve will be proud of its mealtime atmosphere. Campers will enter the dining hall in orderly fashion, accepting their food with gratitude and respect. I have shared more pleasant camp meals than the above-described kind. It's all a matter of leadership.

Some camps allow random seating for meals, encouraging cabin groups to mix. Counselors are placed halfway down the table rather than at one end, permitting greater ease in maintaining order. Each table becomes an island of pleasant conversation, with *please* and *thank you* punctuating requests. Too idealistic? Not when the value of mealtime is recognized.

Where family-style service is practiced, some campers will need help with the size of portions, so that the dish serves everyone at the table. Requiring that campers eat a little of everything, including foods they do not like, is unkind. Camp is no place to try to alter lifelong tastes.

Campers should be expected to eat what they take and make no complaints about what they do not like. Watch for the camper who eats little except desserts, then fills up on goodies from the canteen! Ordinarily the canteen is not opened after mealtime except for nonfood items.

Listless eaters may be ill. Alert the camp nurse to any you suspect may not be eating properly. Balanced, satisfying meals ward off most common health complaints, and wise leaders know that good food is the camp's best promotional expenditure.

Occasionally you will find an epidemic of appetite-destroying comments or stories springing up. You will eliminate these, along with food-wasting pranks. Campers who create undue disturbance should quietly be corrected, not by a counselor bellowing from the far end of the table. It is a general rule that campers will act as rowdy as leaders permit, and where mealtime is bedlam, leaders must assume the blame.

Many camps recognize the hand-raised signal for quiet. A public address system, where one is needed, is kept at minimum volume, never turned up to outshout the campers. Background music is mainly a nuisance. The finest music is the happy murmur of relaxed campers enjoying the fellowship around the table, a primary exercise in Christian fellowship.

Mealtime provides opportunity for several lighter activities: fun songs, mail call, awards, special recognitions, and *brief* announcements or introductions. Keep after-meal programs short. The dining hall crew must begin preparations for the next meal.

ALL-CAMP MEETINGS

Most camps offer one or more daily all-camp meetings for worship, evangelism, missionary presentations, or Bible study. You can help make these meetings a rewarding experience rather than a battle of wits between leader and camper. Ultimately, the program bears the responsibility for maintaining camper interest, but your presence will help. A dozen counselors warming the back row has little value. Scattered among the campers, the same counselors spread serenity, particularly when a counselor invites himself to sit next to a chronic disturber. Interested, participating counselors beget attentive chapel worship.

Your presence in chapel has other values. Knowing what your campers are learning provides points of contact for cabin devotions and personal counsel. If you have the privilege of teaching a cabin Bible study, you can relate your study to other camping teaching.

As you share group worship, you will want to be alert for spiritual responses among campers. Some who will not respond in traditional ways will reveal concern by facial expression. You may find them open to conversation following the meeting. Campfires often offer opportunities for helping campers make spiritual discoveries. Something about the outdoor campfire and the darkness knits campers and leaders together. Today's world offers precious few such moments.

Your role during all-camp programs is to help campers gain maximum value from whatever activity is available. Nowhere is the counselor more important than during all-camp worship and Bible study.

BEACH, BALL FIELD, AND CRAFTS

Recreation and free periods create varied opportunities for service. Your cabin group demands first loyalty. Is there a boy or girl who needs encouragement? Perhaps a shy youngster longs for a boat ride, but he doesn't qualify unless a counselor goes along. Simple crafts look bewildering to young campers. You can minister to your campers in many ways.

But is this ministering? Are genuine spiritual values found in boats and camp crafts? Consider the counselor who lost his temper when the umpire called him out on strikes. Some dramatic teaching took place concerning the spiritual grace of sportsmanship, though on the negative side! Another counselor comforted a boy who had dropped a fly ball, thus losing the game for his team. That moment of comfort was a lesson in Christian love the boy will never forget.

Many a camper remembers an afternoon when his counselor quietly shared the wonders of God's love as they sat together braiding a lanyard. Whenever you touch the life of a camper, you minister. God's Spirit may speak to an individual at any moment of the day or night.

Sharing in all-camp recreation periods also adds a safety factor to camp. Swimming is quite safe when a sufficient number of mature persons are on hand to aid the lifeguard. Boating, canoeing, sailing—whenever campers are on the water, great care must be exercised. Dangerous horseplay is minimized when adults are on the scene. While you help your campers enjoy camp adventures, you help keep them safe.

The degree of emphasis on competitive sports varies according to camp traditions and campers' ages. Everyone who wishes to play should be encouraged, but reluctant participants should seldom be forced. Proper rules and techniques should be taught. Serving a volleyball looks simple, but remember the first time you tried?

The rifle and archery range attract wide camper interest requiring experienced leadership, both to maintain safety and to teach skills. Random shooting is never permitted, nor are campers ever allowed on the ranges without supervision. Safety must constantly be stressed in all activity. A flying baseball bat is potentially as deadly as an arrow. You help keep camp safe by mingling with your campers.

You should not feel hesitant to participate in an activity where you are not skilled. Beating the counselor in a game is exhilarating to a camper, and not the least bit harmful to the camper-counselor relationship. It helps a camper to discover that adults sometimes lose.

As camps develop more diversified programs, you will find many opportunities to become a learner with your campers. Several activities for campers with special interests have been established: drama, photography, the arts, music. You can help your campers grow through new experiences, and perhaps grow yourself.

I have been disturbed to note how many camps fail to mark playing fields. While a choose-up ball game in a pasture with stumps and anthills for bases can do in an emergency, you can forestall many arguments with a sack of lime and a measuring tape.

THE MOMENTS BETWEEN

Elective approaches to camp programming are becoming increasingly common. What do you do when a campr elects to do nothing? We are learning that some young people want time to think, that idleness is not necessarily evidence of indifference. Quiet, serious-minded campers tend to be neglected in favor of the outgoing youngster who drags the counselor off to the rifle range. Watch for the camper who seems uninvolved, but don't force activity when the camper's desire may be time to think.

Tensions between campers develop in the moments between activities. Waiting for meals produces more than the usual share of squabbles, and that is a good time to make your presence felt.

Remember that God works all the time, not just during chapel or campfire. Deeper concerns burn in young hearts than many adults realize. As a counselor, you will have the privilege of sharing sacred moments if you keep alert and sensitive to campers' moods. Maintain an open, approachable spirit throughout the day.

THE WILDERNESS WAY

For generations the natural environment was largely ignored as a program feature by Christian camp leaders. The beach and ballfield provided most of the recreation, with campers engaged in sports much like those they enjoyed at home. Outpost camping (cabin groups tenting on a remote corner of the campsite) was rare. Nature trails rarer still. Wilderness skills were almost never cultivated, and such activity as canoe trips or backpacking were viewed with suspicion and sometimes hostility. How could Christian camping be conducted so far from the chapel?

But nature lovers and wilderness-minded men and women prevailed, and today's campers find activity quite different from their school playground. Many camps are blessed with a naturalist, amateur or professional, like Camper Charlie.

Old Camper Charlie loved to spin yarns about Dan'l and the Boone girls, Flora and Fauna. While his imagination often outstripped fact, Charlie's love for nature and his concern that the pioneer spirit be kindled in young hearts added a rich element to camp life. Camp programs should, as far as possible, be built around activities campers do not ordinarily enjoy at home.

Since most campers come from urban and suburban homes, the camp's natural setting offers a variety of program opportunities. Yet too many camps still limit recreation to the ball field and volleyball court. To be sure, some camps are more suited than others to a nature program, but I never visited a camp yet that did not have trees, sky, birds, and a patch of ground where cookouts and overnights could be held.

Camp-Outs And Hikes

Junior campers do not demand Alaskan wilderness to enjoy outdoor experiences. A circle of tents in the far corner of camp blends with childhood's imagination to provide memorable adventure, especially if the hike to the tent site winds along the lake, through the lush growth of the swamp, along the fence, and finally to the high ground where the tents wait to be pitched. With a little planning, you can lay out a challenging hiking trail on a few acres of land.

But why bother? Surely cabins are more comfortable than

tents! Why disrupt the schedule for a silly walk through the woods? That's comfort-loving adult talk. Carried to its logical conclusion, the whole camp idea is a bother. Why not simply haul kids to church and play ball in the parking lot between classes?

Christian camping provides a real-life experience for youth in an outdoor setting where spiritual discovery takes place, not only during structured teaching sessions, but through every moment. You have heard many times that salvation is *caught*, not taught. That's why the camp program can offer any activity of interest to campers, and the tradition of Dan'l Boone surely holds interest!

I am encouraged to note the growth of wilderness trips sponsored by Christian camps for older campers. I have more to say about this in another book, *The Wilderness Way.* But there's no reason younger campers should be deprived of wilderness adventure in the camp's backyard, where they can be taught basic camping skills, which will generate interest in greater adventures to come. Building a fire, pitching a tent, paddling a canoe, or riding a horse require about the same skill in any setting. A graded campcraft achievement program would delight young pioneers.

NATURE DISCOVERY

Specialization has come to camp, and the campcraft specialist may assume major responsibility for planning nature hikes and campouts. But you should be prepared to share adventure with your cabin group. The outpost campfire before bedtime may prove to be the high point of the week, a time of genuine spiritual discovery.

Campouts allow for other kinds of discovery too. Many youngsters know practically nothing about nature; trees, for example. One child reported, "There are two kinds of trees. Christmas trees and the other kind." Campers seldom take kindly to learned lectures on the classification of shrubs and trees complete with Latin nomenclature. But they do appreciate knowing the difference between a cedar and a spruce, between a maple and an aspen. Small markers at eye level along the nature trail will not defile the forest and will enrich the camper's store of nature lore.

I recall a boy staring in awe at the Wyoming skies one night. The stars shone brightly in the moonless night, more stars than the boy imagined there could be. City lights and smog blur the heavens and blur the spirit too. Up there in the mountains all was clear.

Why not familiarize yourself with the major constellations and point them out to your campers? Surely every youngster should know how to locate the North Star. In these days of astronauts and space exploration, the grandeur of the heavens should be taught.

For many years leaders at one camp lamented the presence of a bog which bred mosquitos and took up valuable camp acres. A total waste of land, they felt. Then an imaginative leader came along. He consulted authorities and learned how the bog could be developed into a wetlands nature center, with discovery trails and blinds for observing bird life.

Another camp converted a slough into a small lake, stocking it with pan fish to the campers' delight. Many camps located close to public lands can add hiking and camping to their programs. Campcraft can be taught in any area where small fires can safely be allowed. You will discover that cooking outdoors demands little more than indoor cooking: a secure place for pots and pans, control of the heat source, and proper ingredients in the pot. That's all there is to it! Practice at home over a backyard fire.

Some campers will delight in bird study. Probably scores of different kinds of birds frequently visit your camp. Why not create a birds-we-have-seen chart for your cabin or recreation room? But be prepared for early morning hikes if your campers get bit by the bird-watching bug!

PIONEERING TODAY

Now a word about the pioneering skills and camp kinks which inevitably find their way into camp books. The day has passed for the indiscriminate cutting of trees and shrubs for pioneering crafts. Lashing, for example, is a challenging skill, but hardly practical today. The woven-twig roasters for broiling fish or steaks which you see pictured in books make far better pictures than cooking utensils. If you don't believe me, try making one that works!

The rule today is, never cut a growing shrub or tree or disturb the soil more than is absolutely necessary. This eliminates ditching tents (digging a narrow trench along each side for water to drain), a practice which usually fails anyhow. With millions of people using the wilderness each year, a new conservation philosophy has arisen. In most forest areas, the law forbids cutting live growth.

A simple fire grate propped up on stones is superior to the pole between two crotched sticks beloved by campcraft illustrators, though I confess a bent toward building a tripod for hanging pots over the fire when dead poles of proper size can be found. Fire holes are nonsense when you think about it. Fire demands oxygen and how do you ventilate a hole? Build the smallest possible fire, scraping down to mineral soil. Replace humus and turf after the fire is extinguished. Generally, designated fire areas are provided.

Today's goal for trail campers requires great care to restore the campsite to its natural state. Even the ashes remaining after the fire is thoroughly soaked and cold are scattered so that the next camper can scarcely find where the fire had been. This applies of course to camps in areas where permanent fireplaces to not exist.

Garbage, bottles, cans and other leftover debris must not be buried or disposed of in the lake, as was once the custom. Every vestige of camp life should be removed, either by burning or packing out. Where permanent overnight campsites are used, the woodsman's code requires that you leave a decent supply of firewood for the next camper, and prop tent poles and stakes in plain view for the next campers.

Practice these principles on all hikes and campouts, even though the camp maintenance truck will be by later. Teach campers to care for their world, and to preserve it for those who will come along later.

Campcraft and nature-lore should never degenerate into an academic exercise. There's hardly a camper alive who wants to attend nature "class." Younger campers look forward eagerly to a hike, campout, cabin cookout or fishing contest. They will learn by observing and doing. And if there's an award for achievement, most campers will work more diligently.

Camp zoos trouble me because the incarcerated creatures look so unhappy. Why not a gallery of photographs showing animals commonly found near camp? The zoo encourages campers to capture pet frogs, snakes, turtles, and lizards, rendering your life less peaceful.

More animals share the camp than you probably imagine. Rabbits, squirrels, chipmunks, and mice are common. Raccoons, skunks, and maybe a black bear may visit during the night. Fox, deer, beaver, muskrats, weasels, and mink make their homes in forests, fields, and waterlands near many camps. Since most animals prefer night feeding, campers seldom see them; but their homes and footprints, and the evidence of their work, can be discovered and identified.

Meanwhile, back at the camp, Marsha and Willie race toward Marsha's counselor.

"It was so," pants Marsha.

"It was not," Willie insists. "It was too big."

"I saw the yellow mark on its throat, and it was just the right size," Marsha argues.

"Too big," replies Willie.

Miss Counselor produces a brightly-illustrated booklet and Marsha turns triumphantly to the page describing the yellowthroated warbler. "See?"

Willie grudgingly admits defeat, and Marsha gains the honor of entering Bird #27 on the official camp bird roster.

A camper may inform you that there are *millions* of different kinds of insects, a fact you never doubted. He may add that scientists have identified more than 15,000 different kinds of ants and invite you to inspect the official camp anthill just behind the craft building.

Inside the building, you will discover why the campers are alive to nature. Leatherwork and craftstrip still find their place, but your eye is arrested by patterns for simple bird-houses (which houses adorn the trees around camp). A girl sorts leaf specimens preparatory to making spatter prints. Another girl arranges dried grasses and seedpods into an artistic display.

Lodge and cabin walls are decorated with leaf specimens, insect collections, full-color bird pictures, a great paper-wasp nest, and the handiwork of a beaver. The woodsmanship group discusses conservation, practices proper use of compass and ax. They master a half-dozen knots, and learn to cook outdoors, with or without utensils. Posters from forestry and conservation offices create more atmosphere.

Of course the ball field is properly marked, as are the horseshoe pits and the volleyball court. Campers shoot baskets and play table tennis. Different campers respond to different activities, and whenever campers enjoy themselves in wholesome play, camp is attaining its objectives. Camp must be fun, and part of your task as a counselor is to help campers enjoy all that camp offers by sharing adventure with them.

References to nature abound in the Bible. Jesus taught from flowers, rocks, sheep, and rain. David saw the glory of God in the heavens. Read the Sermon on the Mount and underline all references to nature. You'll be surprised! Consider the lessons drawn from sparrows, eagles, ants, and the thirst of a deer (hart). If any aspect of camp programming merits special attention, surely nature study qualifies. Considering the rich nature content of the Bible, can we afford to ignore the creation?

You might not share Camper Charlie's love for Dan'l Boone, but you may discover an open door to the heart of many campers through broader use of nature study and campcraft. Who knows what God's Spirit might accomplish in a wooded corner of the camp?

5

Cloudy in the West

Every camp leader dreams of that week when the sun shines every day, the temperature remains at 72 degrees, and the wind blows just enough to discourage the flies and mosquitos. Such weeks are rare! The dream includes a week free from accidents, illnesses, and weeping campers longing to go home. The wise leader tempers dreams with cold reality. And cold it might become!

WEATHER PROBLEMS

The ominous news from the weather forecaster declares rain for Thursday. That's picnic day plus the all-camp olympics! Rain may come. Chilly weather may close the waterfront. A heat wave creates other problems. The schedule lies shattered at the counselor's feet.

But weather variations are normal. Football fans sit through rain, sleet, and snow. October hayrides are usually cold, but who cares? Weather is but a circumstance, not a crippling calamity. There's no use denying that camper morale sags as the rain continues to drum on cabin roofs. But almost anyone can lead campers in the sunshine! Foul weather puts you to the test, a test you will flunk if you don't prepare.

Preparing begins with your attitude. If you allow weather to determine your mood, you're doomed to a life of misery, for rain is inevitable. So determine to keep your spirits high, rain or shine!

Most camps stand ready to assist you through planned rainy day programs. Indoor recreation areas not needed during sunny days are pressed into service. Perhaps the fireplace is kindled. Table-game tournaments flourish. Impromptu amateur shows are scheduled, or the stunt-skit night is moved up. If adequate planning has been done, rain can be almost fun.

Many activities continue as scheduled, with meaningful features added. Chapel and classes meet; meals are served on time, with a bit of extra programming following. The rained-out campfire may be held inside, with or without a fireplace, followed by hot chocolate or popcorn. But outdoor recreation and craft hours remain to be filled, probably through your imagination.

If the temperature has not dropped severely, try a hike, even for those without rain gear. I hear a cry of alarm, "They'll catch cold!" Not likely. Colds are caught from people, not rain. Germs cause colds, and a rain hike is quite germ free. A severe chill might have some deleterious effect on health, though I can muster some forty years of early-season trout fishing to debate the point. A brisk hike in the rain, followed by a shower or toweling and a change of clothes, can't help but improve camp life. But probably the nurse will out-vote me.

Barring cold or lightning, there is no reason why campers should not be allowed to swim in the rain.

Weather should be viewed as a challenge, not a calamity. When rain begins during the night, the program may be moved back an hour or more to allow the campers extra sleep time. But be ready for surplus energies when night falls!

The movie and filmstrip projector come in handy when it rains. Ordinarily, camp programming avoids duplication with activity commonly enjoyed at home; but under the proper circumstances, films can provide wholesome diversion.

Write out plans for at least one full day of bad weather. Collect a story or two, if you will be serving younger campers. Plan folk singing for older campers. As much as I dislike parlor games, you may find several that will amuse your campers. You might invite a neighbor cabin over for the afternoon.

List topics that will stir discussion among campers. Devise

simple games and contests. A golf match can be conducted with the use of paper plates (holes in the center) inverted at various spots in the cabin. A small rubber ball propelled by a narrow board completes the equipment. Even old-fashioned hopscotch is not to be scorned.

The secret for rainy-day success lies in variety. Always try to change activities just before interest lags. The grimmest test for counselors comes when the rain persists day after day, as sometimes it will.

Doctor In The Crowd?

Problems other than rain can shatter camp morale for the individual, the cabin group, or the whole camp. Enjoying camp depends upon feeling well. As a counselor, your campers' health is of prime concern. Illness takes many forms. Hurt feelings can be as painful as a stomach-ache, perhaps more so. Few aches exceed the pain of homesickness. And don't ignore the lovesick!

Never ignore an injury or complaint of pain. Let the camp nurse determine the seriousness of the problem. Never apply a bandage or administer an aspirin without the nurse's supervision, unless you are away from camp on an extended outing. Take injured or ill campers to the nurse personally, or place them in the custody of a responsible staff person. Let the nurse remove slivers and drain blisters.

Keep alert to symptoms of illness. Nausea, dizziness, stomach pains, headaches, loss of appetite, flushed face, paleness, lethargy, short temper. Any persistent irregularity in appearance or conduct calls for consultation with the nurse.

Never leave an ill camper alone. The camp infirmary accommodates campers who need special care. Never excuse a camper from meals or activity on the grounds of illness. Insist that the nurse make this decision. While serious camp illnesses are not common, you share the responsibility for maintaining health standards.

A knowledge of first aid may prove vital if the nurse is not readily available, or if you are away from camp on an outing.

An injured camper should not be moved until professional help has come, unless it is necessary to save his life. Mouth-to-mouth resuscitation should be mastered as the best method for reviving victims where breathing has stopped. Severe bleeding must be arrested and breathing restored or death quickly ensues, but most other conditions can wait the arrival of medical help. C.P.R. is offered in many training programs.

Unless there is reason not to alter an injured person's position, ease him onto a blanket or coat and keep him lying down, his head slightly lower than his body, his feet elevated twelve to eighteen inches. Keep him warm, though avoid overheating. Allow him to drink if he is conscious. Reassure him that help is coming, and keep curious onlookers away.

Persons injured in diving accidents should be removed from the water on a flat, rigid surface, since veterbrae may have been damaged, and improper handling can paralyze or kill the victim. Watch for shock in all accidents. Shock can kill, even when injury is minor.

Review camp health policies. Check your campers for regular bowel movements. Remind them that all medications should be administered by the nurse, even those they bring with them. Immediately report all injuries, no matter how slight, to protect the camper and the camp.

THE HOMESICK

Young campers often experience homesickness. Most recover and stay through the week, but a few cannot master their illness. And it is a genuine illness, though of psychological origin. As far as I know, it has never been fatal. Ridiculing the homesick is heartless, but yielding to the camper's wish to go home is not always best. Homesickness grows out of insecurity and fear, and sooner or later a child must learn to survive away from parents and home, so you will do the camper a favor if you can help him stay.

Suggest some area of unusual interest—a horseback ride, for example. Assure the camper that homesickness happens to most people, and that it will go away. Avoid a phone call home if possible; the mother may be suffering child sickness, and both will end up bawling!

Enlist the help of a woman staff member for a homesick boy, and try to resolve the problem before nightfall! Homesickness is contagious! Darkness intensifies loneliness, and a child crying in the cabin can unnerve marginal cases. You might have quite a night.

Make it seem difficult for the child to be released from camp. As a last resort, allow him to phone home, with the information that his parents will have to arrange travel. If there is no relief, you will simply have to allow a homesick camper to leave. A homesick child can become physically ill. Even though this may not happen, camp will be a week-long nightmare, a memory of horror.

Offer love and affection, and commend the homesick to the loving Saviour. Homesickness to a little camper is about as bad an illness as he can know.

The Lovesick

Occasionally you may have to deal with a love-sick camper. This transient surge of emotion often fastens on an unsuspecting adult, perhaps you.

Lovesickness seems to afflict girls more often than boys, or perhaps girls are more expressive. At any rate, the condition exists. Though childhood crushes are shortlived and usually harmless, they are very real. In spite of every caution not to tamper with the mysterious emotional moods of childhood, the problem must be met when it arises. When you discover one of your campers smitten by another staff person, be careful not to display amusement. Let the camper know that such feelings are common, and that the person they admire is fortunate to be loved. But gently remind the child that these feelings will change in a day or so.

When you are the object of the crush, the problem is a bit more delicate. You might say something like, "Thank you,

Carol (or Johnnie). I'm very happy to have you for one of my best friends. We're going to have a wonderful time in camp this week."

The emotions of a child must be honored, though any response that would encourage the transient feelings is cruel. Never laugh at such a camper. The crush will soon pass, but not the hurt if a confidence is betrayed. If the crush persists, refer the camper to the camp nurse or pastor, someone of the same sex. While pointing out to the afflicted that leaders like all campers equally, you must seek to preserve the dignity of the camper with kindness and understanding.

Mary Loves Joe

Romance in co-ed teen camps must be approached from a wholesome point of view. It is both normal and desirable for young people to discover an increasing interest in each other. Leaders continue to debate the comparative values of one-sex versus co-ed camps. The pattern in some places finds co-ed camping beginning at the high school level, while other regions operate co-ed programs from junior age on up. Several excellent camps serve older boys in specialized camping ministries with no apparent lack of interest because girls are absent. All-girl camps also report good results, particularly in trail-camping programs.

The mood of our day and the moral climate of many communities make co-ed camp leaders increasingly aware of incipient dangers. Prospective campers should understand clearly the standards of Christian camping, and those who cannot accept the standards should be encouraged to stay home.

Should Christian camping accept overt courtship as normal social responses among high school campers? Not in my opinion. Warm friendships, wholesome affection, and companionship do not dilute the spiritual atmosphere. But counselors should pass the word quietly and firmly when acceptable standards are violated.

Some camp leaders play up boy-girl interests in a childish fashion, which is demeaning to the campers. This occurs often

in junior-high camps, where the campers already lack sufficient maturity to relate to one another in a meaningful way.
Silly allusions to love and romance only magnify the problem.

Helping campers accept their God-given sexuality, and inte-
grate this life-force into their Christian experience, is one of
camping's great ministries. Openness and honesty with campers will accomplish far more than impossible rules. Overt vio-
laters of good taste should be approached by camp leaders
with kind but firm alternatives. Accept the camp standards or
go home. Sometimes staff members must be reminded too!

TRAGEDY

Dark clouds of tragedy can destroy a camp more quickly
than rain, yet tragedy is possible whenever people engage in
the kinds of activity found in camp. Morality as well as the
law require adequate standards for health and safety in all
camp programs. Even where trained, responsible leadership is
provided, tragedy may strike.

The amazing fact is that so few deaths or major injuries
occur in Christian camps, in spite of the millions of campers
who participate each year. But one death is too many, if that
death resulted from carelessness. Negligence has cost some
camps their property, and left lifetime scars on the conscience
of leaders.

Should a death or serious injury occur, the counselor should
not communicate with anyone beyond securing help. The
camp director is the spokesman for the camp, and he will
make a full report of the accident. You will report to him your
involvement, supplying names of witnesses and every known
factor. Do not attempt to speak for the camp to authorities or
bystanders.

Campers should be removed immediately from an accident
scene. Tragedy is loaded with peril, for mass hysteria can
sweep through the camp. It is generally best to deal with
campers in cabin groups rather than in a general assembly.
Then, as soon as possible, resume normal camp activity. This
in no way shows disrespect for the victim.

Direct conversation away from the accident, and avoid speculation. Facts should be frankly shared, and the gravity of an accident truthfully reported. When a death has occurred, the cause should be explained as soon as it is known. Blame-fixing must not be allowed.

A brief, comforting reading of Scripture and prayer will soothe fears. Camp should rarely be closed because of tragedy unless the event completely devastates morale, for no good cause can be served. It is the director's duty to notify the parents of an accident victim and determine any adjustments in camp schedules.

Above all, shun the temptation to rationalize tragedy by suggesting that God allowed it to happen for some spiritual purpose. Campers may indeed be moved to make decisions because of the tragedy, but to excuse a death on that premise is ignoble. Most camp leaders serve a lifetime without this sad experience, but tragedy can strike at any time. Prepare yourself in prayer for such a possibility, and be ready to stand by your campers.

EVACUATION, SEARCH, AND RESCUE

Some camps have worked out evacuation procedures, should any circumstance make it necessary to move campers in a hurry. Forest fires, floods, tornadoes, even earthquakes in some regions, make it vital to have such a plan. All staff members should be aware of the plan, and how they should function when the evacuation decision is made. While the need may never arise, adequate preparation could save lives.

Search and rescue plans have been readied for camps in wilderness areas. Ordinarily, campers will not be employed in off-grounds activity, but a search plan covering the camp area can prove vital. A tag left behind on the buddy board by a forgetful camper can give the lifeguard anxious moments. He has no alternative but to assume the person is in the lake. A pre-planned search can comb the camp in a matter of minutes, and usually the forgetful camper will be located, even while a search of the swimming area is under way. Brief your campers on their responsibilities for search and rescue. All camps should conduct fire drills in buildings where large numbers gather. Review procedures with your campers should a fire break out in the cabin.

Campers should be drilled on the necessity for safety. Most camp tragedies can be traced at least in part to camper carelessness. Parents and churches entrust young people to camp leaders, assuming they will exercise every possible caution to return the campers safely home. No unnecessary risks should be taken, and prayers should ascend daily for divine protection.

6

May I See You—Alone?

CAMP COUNSELING is more than maintaining order and playing games. The counselor's duties are many and varied, all of them directed toward one goal: fulfilling the objectives of Christian camping in the camper's life. You will face some responsibilities confidently, others fearfully. But the one responsibility you should determine to master is the art of counseling individuals, for your greatest ministry lies here.

When we attach the word "counseling" to a conversation between two persons, the image arises of an austere office with a couch. This is unfortunate. Counseling is mostly caring and listening. No magic formula exists that will dissolve every personal problem campers bring to camp. Counseling individuals never ceases to be an adventure, and as often as not, you will come from the counseling opportunity unsure of the results. Professional counselors readily confess a meager batting average, if success means a complete cure. However, there are principles which enable you to be of some help to most campers and of significant help to many.

The Anatomy Of Counseling

The two organs most important in counseling are the heart and the ear, in that order. Love and listening. Too many counselors seem to think the brain and the tongue are most important. The most dangerous animal most campers will ever encounter is the eager-beaver, amateur-psychiatrist counselor; the one who has read a few books and taken a course or two in psychology.

Books are fine, and you should read as many as possible. But I hope you will major in the Book, where you'll find more common sense help in counseling than in all the other texts put together. Jesus loved people, and He listened to them. He often met problems with a question. He allowed people to discover their own needs by the response His questions drew forth.

There is no substitute for genuine compassion, which is another word for love. Compassion never turns kids off, never half-listens, never says, "That reminds me of the time. . . ." Compassion understands that every camper has great potential for good. Compassion accepts mean campers, sullen campers, lying campers, and thieves. Compassion understands that every act has a cause, a cause that may baffle the wrongdoer more than the counselor.

Compassion refuses to be shocked. Campers rarely confess sins that the counselor is not capable of committing, and probably has committed in one degree or another. Campers seldom use a word that the counselor has not heard before. Bad books, wicked deeds, hypocrisies, drink, tobacco, drugs, immorality; they are as common as humanity. It's useless to tell an offender simply to quit sinning. Most of them would gladly quit if they could.

A lad approached me one August morning after camp Bible study. "Can I talk with you, Cap?" We found a quiet corner. He talked about generalities for a while, about the Bible study just ended. Then he got down to his problem. What did I think about a friend of his who pretended to be a Christian, yet he habitually stole?

"What do you steal?" I asked. I could see denial building in the boy's eyes as he searched mine. Then he spread his hands in despair. Mostly he stole small parts for his model-car hobby. Even when he had the money in his pocket, he stole. Why?

Stealing is a common crime, probably exceeded only by lying as a sin practiced by Christians. We usually rationalize stealing and lying into pious oblivion, but this lad had the courage to face his problem and talk about it. He talked for a long time, telling again and again how foolish and petty his thefts were. "Why do I do it?" he asked.

I could only answer, "I don't know." I lacked the training to unravel the complexities of a personality that found it necessary to steal. Certainly it was pointless to tell the boy to quit stealing. He wanted to quit, but how? What he needed was my heart and ear; so I cared and listened and counted it a privilege. After we prayed together, for the boy was a genuine Christian, he said, "Thanks, Cap. You've helped me a lot." I hadn't said ten sentences in an hour.

The healing power of listening is well known, but we're slow to practice it. It's easier to talk than listen. Honest listening demands discipline, both of brain and tongue.

Listening is the other end of confession. A mysterious therapy flows out of sharing needs. There is little cleansing apart from confession. Effective counseling partakes somewhat of the atmosphere of the confessional. As you listen, you heal. When you have lived among your campers in such a manner that one will share his deepest secrets, you have reached the pinnacle.

Listening is essential, because the real need seldom emerges right away. The camper tests the water with a mild sin to discover how chilly your response will be. If you jump on that problem, you will fail. If you listen with compassion and acceptance, the camper will likely go on, probably still skirting his real burden. He cannot be completely honest until he feels secure. He must be confident that you will not reject him when you learn his most grievous sin.

All of us have a built-in scale of wickedness from gray to black. Your scale may differ from the camper's. Puffing a cast-off cigarette may hardly call for penance on your scale, but a junior camper steeped in the antismoking tradition may feel such a sin nearly unpardonable. Never treat a confession lightly, for conscience is a delicate instrument, and quite readily manipulated. Compassion and listening—even in matters that seem trivial—can bring comfort to a youthful confessor.

HELPING CAMPERS SOLVE COMMON NEEDS

So far we have considered counseling in relation only to sin problems. But don't expect a rash of confessions, and don't attempt to precipitate confessions through a contrived emotional climate. Campers have been known to vie for the most lurid confession! We glamorize sin by making heroes of great sinners who become converted. It takes as much grace to save a child as a drug addict, only childhood conversions do not make effective posters. Most personal counseling opportunities will relate to fairly simple matters. Some of them will be little more than the camper's desire for personal attention, and there's nothing wrong with that. Make your heart and ear available. That's why you're in camp.

Personal counseling aims at helping campers discover their problems and voluntarily apply a solution. Counseling is not advice-giving. Some situations will suggest an obvious course of action, and you should not hesitate to be directive. Should a camper finish school? Of course! But if he seriously asks that question, you can be almost sure you haven't heard the real problem.

Forcing a response on a camper rarely achieves much good, such as compelling one camper to apologize to another. Mere words mean nothing. Bringing a camper to a point where he sees he has hurt someone, so that his apology is sincere, blesses everyone. Most useless is that strange practice of forced public confession. When public confession comes spontaneously, everyone gains.

You will discover books that talk about *directive* and *nondirective* counseling. The distinction is fairly obvious. Using the Bible wisely permits you to be directive and nondirective at the same time. The more you know the Bible, the better able you will be to help campers. When a camper accepts the authority of Scripture, you have but to help him search the Word. Jesus said, "The Law. What does it say?"

If a camper rejects the authority of the Bible, you have another problem, and you must judge when the situation demands directive counseling. Sin is sin no matter what an individual chooses to believe. But unless the camper *voluntarily* accepts your directive, not much is gained. Your purpose is not to win arguments over moral or practical issues, but to change lives. Lasting change is achieved through the spirit of the person who voluntarily accepts change.

In a sense, changing campers is what Christian camping is for; changing unconverted campers to Christians, changing disobedient Christians to committed Christians, changing the direction of aimless Christians. All learning involves some change, and accomplishing real change is a complicated matter. Don't mistake conformity with change. Many "camp decisions" are nothing more than bowing to a custom the camper understands to be expected of him. Change originates within, and your best opportunity to achieve change is through person-to-person encounters.

Almost any kind of personal contact is good. Don't hesitate to schedule interviews, but don't expect too much from them. If the camp requires written evaluations, tell your campers so. Tell them that a copy of the report will be sent to their home churches. The advantages of such an announcement are obvious!

One of the advantages is the necessity for time alone with each camper, even though the counselor-initiated interview is ordinarily the least productive. Expect premeditated responses, the kind a camper thinks will look good on his "report card." But if you obey the heart-ear law, you can glean valuable insights.

Another personal encounter opportunity grows out of achievement programs. Bible memory, crafts, nature projects, skills; whatever brings camper and counselor together holds promise for useful exchange. But don't forget to listen.

The traditional evangelistic interview offers the most rewarding and the most dangerous counseling situation you will face. Any method you may discover that confronts a camper with the biblical provision for personal salvation is worthy, but beware of systems that impose ideas on a camper, or put words in his mouth. Let the Holy Spirit work. Someone has said, "We win people, the Holy Spirit wins souls."

Soul-winning is the work of God in the truest sense, and we dare not intrude. We can declare what God has said, and what God requires, but beware of imposing assurance on an unsure heart.

I hope the day never comes when evangelistic invitations cease in our camps. While public invitations suitable for older youth and adult audiences require modification for smaller children, campers should be afforded an opportunity to respond to the urgings of the Spirit. You should be prepared to help.

In all learning, there is a mysterious moment of acceptance, blending of mind and will that opens the understanding to a new idea. This is supremely so in the discovery of spiritual truth. Unless God works, nothing happens. Mass appeals demand scrupulous care with children, yet every evidence of interest demands personal attention, regardless of the age. You become the catalyst, and you never share a more sacred moment, nor one more to be coveted, than when a spirit is newborn. Be alert day and night for opportunities to lead campers to Christ, the ultimate experience of a counselor.

A sad remark heard sometimes in evangelistic services goes like this: "We'll sing one more verse, and then the invitation will close." This is blind presumption. Man cannot determine when God will touch a heart, and it is no affront to the preacher if a person is not prepared to respond at that moment. Chrisitan camping opens unlimited opportunities for evangelistic interviews. I reject the proposition that one hour is more suited for salvation than another.

A wooded trail, a fallen tree, a great rock along the shoreline; wherever the camper may be when that mystic moment of acceptance comes, that is the right time. Do not hesitate to ask a camper concerning the state of his soul. Either he is saved or he isn't. Buy up every opportunity to point campers to Christ, but beware of psychological pressure.

CHART AND COMPASS

The proper use of Scripture in counseling insures lasting

benefits. I have stated that quoting "Thou shalt not steal" to a confessed thief has little value and imparts no new information. But having him read 1 John 1:9 offers a base for a new beginning, and opens the way for him to follow in the spirit of Zacchaeus (Luke 19:8).

The broader your knowledge of the Bible, the greater your strength in counseling. One Scripture promise relevant to the camper's need is worth more than a dozen psychological explanations. Encourage the camper to read and interpret the verses. Say to the camper, "On the basis of this promise (command) of God, what do you feel you should do?" A course of action may be obvious to you, and probably to the camper also. Your task is to help the camper adopt the course of his own will.

Know Your Limitations

The camp pastor, program director, or head counselor will be prepared to help with problems that tax your experience and skill. Often you will refer a camper to another staff member for additional counsel.

You may find yourself in deeper water than you can tread. "Margie, I wonder if we shouldn't ask the camp pastor (nurse, head counselor) to help us." Gaining Margie's consent, you will take her to the camp pastor, introduce her, then leave. One counselor at a time is the rule.

Unless you have had adequate training, seek help with complex problems. The intricacies of human personality demand great care lest problems be driven deeper and confusion be multiplied. Ordinarily, camper's burdens will be direct and identifiable. Help them make decisions, but don't decide for them.

Problems For Personal Counseling

What kind of problems can you expect? Probably as many as you have campers. It would be false to suggest that most of your day will be spent unraveling tangled young minds. Yet no part of the counselor's work holds more promise for the camper than the problem-facing session.

Troubled campers must conquer mountains before they can unburden their hearts. First, they fear loss of status in the counselor's eyes (plus a dread that the counselor might tell others). Second, they often believe their problem is peculiar to themselves, in degree if not in kind, bringing the fear that they are abnormal. Third, they have tried to solve the problem before and failed, suggesting hopeless weakness.

We have discussed the week-long opportunity camp affords for building rapport between counselor and camper, and the possibility that a deeply troubled camper will engage in preliminary skirmishes before attacking the real problem. Unless you have known the camper prior to camp, it is unlikely that time will allow the most troublesome concerns to emerge. When you sense serious problems, encourage the camper to seek help. The average camper will open his heart when he learns that you will not reject him because of his problem. Assure him that his problem is common, and that it *can* be solved with God's help.

DESIRE FOR SALVATION

Several methods are available to guide you in leading a camper to a decision for salvation. Study them carefully, but use the Bible throughout the counseling session. As in all good counseling, keep the interview camper-centered. Let the camper read a few verses from the Bible, examining them closely. Do not attempt a sermon on the atonement, or expound on total depravity. Allow the Holy Spirit to apply Scripture to the camper's mind and heart; for unless the Holy Spirit is speaking, your words are useless. If the Spirit is speaking, God's Word is enough. No principle of soul winning is more important than this: base the camper's decision on the promise of God.

Do not force a decision, though you may ask questions that require specific answers concerning Bible verses. Many patterns have been used for dealing with salvation. Most of them include the following concepts:

Everyone needs to be saved
Romans 3:23; Isaiah 53:6

There is only one way to be saved.
John 3:13, 18; Acts 4:12

Jesus saves all who truly believe in Him.
John 1:12, 3:16, 6:37

Salvation means a new life in Christ.
Ephesians 2:8-10; Colossians 3:1

Remember the importance of helping the new Christian confess Christ immediately. Treat every decision with dignity, and particularly the decision for salvation.

Desire For Commitment

A growing spiritual experience demands new points of beginning. Many Christians can point to crisis experiences following salvation. These experiences can be of great significance. Many campers will sense God's leading into a church-related vocation. Again, do not force decisions! Let God speak. You do a great injustice to a young person when you draw from him a pledge of specific service when the conviction of God is not the motivation. There is nothing quite so important to a minister or missionary as the certainty that *God* has called him to his task.

The cumulative effect of a good camp program and the absence of distractions heighten the camper's spiritual perception. Jesus Christ may become more real and more dear than the camper imagined possible. Such experiences are to be cherished. You may have the privilege of sharing sacred moments, and lending lasting beauty, long after the high, holy emotion has passed. Be ready with a bouquet of Bible verses to enrich the hour.

Doubts And Questions

You will learn early in your counseling experience to discern between honest questions and heckling. Youth is the age of doubting, particularly the later teens. How do you know the

Bible is God's Word? What about evolution? Can all the millions of non-Christians be lost? How do you know for sure you have true faith? Kindred questions tumble out faster than you can gather them. The strongest reply possible is your unswerving faith in God and the Bible, even when you must answer, "I don't know how to answer that question." You know God is true because He is real to you. You know the Bible is God's Word because of its effect in your life.

Remember your own struggle toward full confidence in the Scriptures? Perhaps you still experience moments when doubt creeps in. Doubting is the normal reaction of the mind to spiritual truth, for we cannot grasp God's ways without the aid of the Holy Spirit. Young campers who are earnest in their faith still must gain the experience that allows the mind to wrestle with Scripture while the heart remains at peace.

Two special areas you can look for as you work with campers call for care and insight.

HOW CAN I KNOW GOD'S WILL?

No question is more critical for sincere young Christians. You dare not presume on God's domain! Counsel the camper to be faithful in known duties (Bible reading, prayer, witnessing, personal holiness), and assure him or her that God will lead in specific needs. Warn campers that disobedience in everyday Christian requirements precludes any right to God's leading for life's major callings (Proverbs 3:5-6).

Remind your campers that faithful performance at home, church, school and work is required. God generally leads through circumstances, through the counsel of Christian friends, and through the developing awareness of gifts and aptitudes. These are generally more reliable than waiting for a special voice from heaven.

God can and may send a signal to the heart of a Christian by His Spirit, confirming a course of action. This will always be consistent with the Scriptures.

MORAL DIFFICULTIES

Most young people wrestle with basic virtues. Lying, cheating, stealing, and swearing are accepted as indifferent in community and school life. Sexual temptation is aggravated by the stage of physical development campers are experiencing, and by the sensual appeal of many magazines and books.

The high moral claims of Christianity is a whip to the tender conscience of sincere young people, many of whom are gripped by sinful habits before they know the consequences. You will need to teach both God's loving forgiveness and His refusal to countenance sin. Looking around and within may soften your reproach when you hear confessions. While sin is never excused, its presence in young lives can be traced to the greed of the adult world. You are part of a Gideon's tiny band, rescuing God's people from the oppressor.

A comprehensive listing of problems you will face is impossible, and no sure problem-solving formula can be constructed. In every case you must help the camper identify the real problem, evaluate it in the light of Scripture, and to take steps to correct the matter.

Under certain circumstances, you will recognize the need for firm, directive counseling. Campers need to know that authority exists in the Bible, parents, government, camp rules, and basic laws of health and safety. You are obligated to direct a camper into proper paths when his attitude or deeds threaten danger to himself or others.

Years ago I found myself appointed director for the high school week at a small camp. I was new to the area, and I found the staff fearful as night approached. I discovered the lights-out bell traditionally signalled a riot, with cabin raids, pranks, and boys and girls sneaking off into the darkness.

"Why has it been permitted?" I asked. The best answer I could get was "tradition." Apparently each year the campers sought to outdo their predecessors in creating a dangerous moral climate. On several occasions the campers had literally manhandled adult staff members, throwing them in the lake. Little wonder the attendance was small.

While I'm not particularly heroic, I have a sense of responsibility toward campers and their parents. I proposed a drastic remedy which the staff accepted with skepticism. At the campfire I quietly announced that *all* campers would be in their cabins at the lights-out bell, and remain there until morning. I heard a snicker here and there. Then I stated that I would be around shortly after lights-out and require each counselor to report. Any camper absent without valid reason would find his bags packed, and a phone call would be made immediately requesting his parents or pastor to come for him. There were a few sullen stares. We went on with the campfire program.

Not one camper ventured from the cabin after hours. I was prepared to follow through, even to closing down the camp, and the campers sensed this. The staff declared it was the best high school camp they could remember.

While camp is for the camper, it must be managed by leaders who exercise responsible authority to assure the moral and physical safety of the campers. As you counsel individuals, you will help campers to discover solutions to their problems and voluntarily adopt remedies. But you will not hesitate to say "Thus saith the Lord" when the occasion demands.

7

Well, They're Gone

ONE MORNING you'll wake up and discover that camp is over. There were times you thought that day would never come! But it did, and you're both sad and glad. Campers are packing and rolling up sleeping bags. Buses and cars pull into the parking lot. Little brothers and sisters scurry about searching for the right camper. All that remains are good-byes, autographs, and evaluations.

Evaluations preserve the value of camp, so don't treat them lightly! The week you planned so long and worked so hard to accomplish has ended. What really happened? An honest evaluation is not easy, but it is vital. Without evaluation and analysis, camps rarely grow; and campers seldom receive meaningful follow-up.

Not every camp supplies guidelines for evaluation, but if yours does, follow them closely. You will be expected to evaluate your campers and your camp. I would suggest a third area—*self-evaluation*. This may prove the most difficult, but it may be the most important. Self-evaluation permits you to preserve your experiences of the week as a basis for a continuing, growing counseling ministry.

EVALUATING CAMPERS

We looked at factors related to camper decisions in chapter six. We urged you to treat all decisions with dignity. Now you will measure the meaning of decisions as they affected the lives of campers. And you will relay information to the home church or other follow-up persons so that the camper will be encouraged in his new commitment.

Data for your evaluation has been collecting all week in your memory and on scraps of paper, through interviews, and from the observations of others. Specific decisions should be a matter of formal record, of course. Attitudes and responses throughout the week may be less formally noted. Achievements should not be overlooked. Any unusual problems or marks of growth should be noted. A sentence or two interpreting the camper from your viewpoint will prove most helpful. Prepare three copies: one for the camp files, one for the follow-up persons at home, and one for your records. You will find this useful for personal follow-up.

If you have done your job, you will know your campers well, and will have had opportunities to chat with each one privately. You will find a measure of affection for each camper which will tempt you to gloss over certain kinds of information that might cause problems at home. Be objective and honest! A negative report helps concerned persons at home build on your work at camp.

Beware of the temptation to take the camper evaluation reports home under the guise of doing a more thorough job! Compel yourself to wrap up camp work at camp. The kind of person who gives a week to camp rarely goes home to idleness.

Do not hesitate to consult with other staff members. Provide as well-rounded a picture as possible of each camper, including matters which might reflect on your skill. You are not likely to reach every camper equally well.

THE FINAL TOUCH

It is always in order for you to follow up your campers. Camps vary so much in relation to their constituency, it is difficult to suggest one follow-up pattern that works for all. Denominational camps usually draw campers and leaders from a group of churches which maintain close contact through the year, and it is assumed that these churches view the camp as an extension of their ministry and will care for the campers they send.

Agency camps often have a close relationship with the club or society in the camper's home area. But camps may draw campers from many areas, and no single follow-up pattern is possible. Here the camp must look after its campers, or they will be left to drift.

Form letters represent the minimal kind of follow-up. Such a letter is nice to get, and better than nothing, but it's hardly exciting. Often such letters come as Christmas greetings. The best mail follow-up is a personal note from the counselor relating some incident from camp. This demands discipline, as well as records to sort out campers as they merge in memory over the weeks. It would seem tragic if a camper made a decision for Christ, and no one cared enough to let him know he remembers.

Some counselors employ a rest hour to remind the camper of camp. Each camper is provided paper, envelope, and stamp. One rest hour is devoted to writing a letter to tell themselves what camp meant, what decisions were made, or what adventures were enjoyed. The letters are handed to the counselor, who drops them in the mailbox in midwinter.

I recall a letter like that. A boy and his dad from Czechoslovakia had been given temporary lodging in the church, and we sent the boy to camp. Shortly after camp, the father and son left, and we wondered often if their short stay had left an impact. About Christmastime the letter arrived, addressed to Peter. We did not know the forwarding address. I opened the letter and read, "Yesterday I accept Jesus as my Saviour. I am glad."

Prayer remains your constant follow-up privilege. Some campers you will never forget. Others you must add to your prayer list as a reminder. As you pray, your ministry continues. Perhaps someday the Holy Spirit will nudge you to pick up the phone and call a lad working in a filling station. You have no idea what such a call can mean.

Because camper follow-up is such a vital—and often neglected—matter, we will devote a special section to this topic.

Evaluating The Camp

Camp directors sometimes seek evaluations from varying vantage points. You hold the key view of camp, for you see how the program affects the camper. Again, honesty is demanded. Your candid opinion of high and low points in the week, along with thoughts as to why a program feature failed, will help greatly in planning camps to come. The final test of any program element is this: Did it help achieve the camp's objectives in the camper?

You may detect personnel or facility needs. Ask yourself, "What made my work difficult, or easy?" Did the daily schedule flow smoothly? At what point in the day or week did camper interest sag? When did you feel uncomfortable in leadership? How might camp be enriched through new features or facilities? Was adequate provision made for your personal needs?

A key question for evaluation is this: What pre-camp information did you find lacking that hindered preparation? How could the camp more adequately prepare you for counseling?

You may be encouraged to recommend improvements in the camp. Program specialists will not view camp as you do, so give careful thought to the program as you discover campers relating to it. Since camp is for the camper, put yourself in his or her place and seek ways camp could become more meaningful. The recommendations from counselors provide vital data for camp planners.

Self-Evaluation

Well, how did you do? That's the most difficult evaluation of all. For one thing, we have been urged not to credit self with success. That is unhumble. Everyone wants to do better. Granted. But *did* you do better? Before any evaluation can be made, one must establish criteria for measurement.

Sometimes in my itinerant life I come upon pastors wallowing in the mire of despair. Light is darkness and joy is gall. It's easy to say, "Cheer up, brother! It can't be all that bad." But it is. On man's usual scale of achievement, the poor fellow is absolute zero. What then? I try to provide a new point of reference, one not subject to the whim of cranky deacons or perverse church members. The true index for measuring success is one's standing with God. The man who walks with God can't be defeated.

I can't claim great success for this remedy for pastoral blues, but the truth abides nonetheless. We can't control circumstances, and we can't all win the cleanest cabin award the greatest number of times; but God has provided the potential for walking with Himself. Paul experienced shipwrecks but did not count them defeat.

You were a success if your walk with the Lord became more vital. You can't measure success by the number of prizes your campers won, for you may have had superior or inferior campers. Your success can be discovered only as time goes on, perhaps decades later when the fruit appears from seeds planted by your godly life and consistent love for a camper. Beware of pride in your "decision" box score! Decisions mean many things. Has your concern for campers increased? Do you love God's Word more dearly? Does the time of prayer mean more to you? Are you more keenly aware of your shortcomings? These are the criteria for spiritual success.

Early in this book, I suggested that you live for a time in Romans 12 as a good place to learn how to be a good counselor. Now I would urge you to live for a while in Philippians 3 as the place of self-evaluation. I know there are mysteries there, but you'll find a clearly defined goal. As we establish goals, we can measure progress.

As Paul evaluates his personal assets, he places them in perspective, rejecting what man ordinarily considers to be virtues for the surpassing worth of knowing Christ Jesus. Then Paul takes us deeply into his self-awareness. When you have mastered Philippians 3:10-11, you will be well on your way toward success as a Christian leader. And you will understand Paul's mature humility in the following verses. The goal Paul mentions in verse 14, and the prize, what might they be? Try reading it this way. "I press toward the goal for the prize: the upward call of God in Christ Jesus." The prize is the calling! If during your week at camp you felt the tug of the Spirit to spend yourself to help others Godward, you had a good week.

I have included a self-examination in this chapter. You will want to check up on your grasp of the counseling machinery, and your growth in specific skills. You will note the moments when frustration or anger caused you to fail momentarily. But you will forgive yourself, with the knowledge that, being a mortal, such moments will likely occur again. Only as you grow spiritualy can you strengthen your counseling role. You may not feel content, but press on! Paul had been working at it a good deal longer than you when he wrote Philippians 3.

Twenty Questions For Counselors

Be specific and honest! If you recognize no progress in an area, admit it. And don't accept perfunctory Bible reading and prayer as meaningful devotions, nor mere civility as Christian grace.

Be candid, then forgiving. Only as you look honestly at yourself can you grow. This may be a mental exercise only, but greater value is gained if you write your responses. You will not be required to share your discoveries, but you may uncover pockets of personal need for special prayer work.

1. Has the week at camp enriched my personal devotional life?
2. What significant truth did I gain from Bible reading this week?
3. What prayer burdens were impressed on my heart?
4. Did I maintain my personal devotional life through the week?
5. What counseling interviews did I initiate with my campers?
6. What counseling interviews were initiated by my campers?
7. How thoroughly did I prepare for cabin Bible study and devotions?

8. When did I lose my composure?

9. Which of my campers did I reach most effectively? Least effectively?

10. What made the difference in my effectiveness?

11. What new skills or crafts did I explore this week?

12. What new ideas did I conserve for next year?

13. What points of tension developed in my relations with the camp program?

14. What plans have I made for camper follow-up?

15. How accurate and thorough were my camper evaluations?

16. When did I indulge self-interests rather than serve my campers?

17. When did I initiate service beyond my normal duties?

18. What needs that I might have met did I pass by because they were not my duty?

19. What plans have I made to improve my counseling skills?

20. What names and needs have I added to my prayer list?

NEXT YEAR AND BEYOND

I met a little lady in her 70's a few years ago whose eyes lit up like Christmas when she learned I was a camper. She retreated to her room and returned with a bundle of packages. Each one contained samples of crafts, some showing many years' use. This lady had been a handcraft leader in camps for thirty years, and she was excited about the coming season. She had discovered several new ideas and couldn't wait to share them.

She had been a housewife and mother, but camp was her annual assignment from the Lord. Her scrapbooks and bundles of crafts bore testimony of a ministry worthy of a saint. She never aspired to become the evangelist or director. Her skill was in handcraft and in loving and enjoying campers. I wondered how many thousands of lives were different because of this little lady.

Perhaps the Lord is appointing you to a life of camp counseling. I expect camps will continue as long as the Lord delays His coming, and many of them will depend on volunteer counselors like you. Why not preserve your experiences through a notebook? Good ideas are all around, and the mind easily loses what at the moment seems unforgettable. Counseling becomes exciting when you see it not as a chore but as a ministry.

I have alluded to the importance of books. The final section lists helpful books in several categories of camp activities and includes annotated suggestions. These can guide you to many hours of worthwhile study. As you cultivate personal spiritual growth, work on new activities to create interest among campers. As you read, feed ideas into your notebook.

Growth comes through association with people as well as through reading. Perhaps you serve as a Sunday school teacher, youth worker, or club leader. Training in these areas will strengthen camp work as well. Workshops, seminars, and discussion groups where you share with other leaders stimulate new ideas and provide for growth.

In many areas Christian camp leaders meet regularly for fellowship and sharing. Christian Camping International unites camp leaders around the world, sponsoring national, regional, and sectional conferences. You will find much help here.

As we conclude Unit One, we recognize that just the barest beginning has been made in discussing the counselor's craft. But hopefully these pages have stimulated your thinking and strengthened your resolve to be an effective servant of Christ Jesus among campers. If so, my purpose in writing the book has been realized.

Happy Camping!

UNIT 2

A Deeper Look

Four areas of camp counseling are considered in greater depth in Unit 2. Chapter 8 will encourage counselors to think through the goals of the camp and its ministry. The dramatic nature of camping tempts enthusiastic leaders to forget that camp is not an end in itself, but a means toward the end of reaching people with the gospel. The discussion includes goals for the camper, the camp, the counselor, and a call to excellence.

Chapter 9 probes the question of camp decisions. The material originally made up a booklet entitled *Way to Grow,* but has been included in the *Camp Counselor* because of its critical importance. The nature of spiritual decisions and the possibility of meaningless responses that can harm the camper are explored. The counselor's allies in guiding campers toward meaningful decisions are considered.

Chapter 10 looks at camp study in relation to the counselor. One approach to Bible study and devotions is outlined, with samplings from *Cabin/Trail Devotions,* a camp study method published by Camping Guideposts.

Chapter 11 tackles the toughest question in camping: follow-up. The counselor's potential as the key to effective follow-up is reviewed, along with a discussion of a new approach to contact with campers who make decisions—a take-home study correlated with the camp Bible studies.

8

The Heart of the Matter

ONCE THERE WAS A MAN who desperately wanted to cross the sea. Day and night he dreamed of reaching the other shore, but he had no way to cross. One day someone said, "Why don't you build a boat?" The man began, learning the skills and gathering materials. Slowly his boat took shape, and everyone stopped to admire the workmanship. He proved to be an exceptionally fine boat builder. Even as he worked he thought of improvements, and soon he owned the finest boat on the coast. The last I heard he was still improving his boat. He never put out to sea!

How easily we forget our real goals, a danger camp leaders must constantly face. Christian camping has grown into a powerful instrument for evangelism and Christian education, possessing breadth and flexibility greater than any other kind of spiritual ministry. This sweeping statement probably will not be challenged. Since camping belongs to everyone, no other work is threatened.

Increasingly the church uses camping as a base for outreach and training, with year-around programs becoming the norm. Retreats, leader planning seminars, weekend family camps, lay training institutes—the variety of needs camp can meet seems endless. But the goal remains constant: to win people for Christ and to train Christians in godliness. This is the heart of the matter.

As a camp counselor you fit into the very heart of Christian camping. The burden of Christian camping is to help each camper cross the sea toward the shore of spiritual maturity. We have discussed many systems and techniques to help in this crossing, but beware lest you become so absorbed in building the boat you forget to sail!

GOALS FOR THE CAMPER

The goals for Christian camping are identical with those of the church: to fulfill God's purposes in people. While we talk about evangelism and Christian education as separate concepts, they are in reality inseparable aspects of God's plan. Evangelism seeks to lead campers to that point where they accept God's gift of salvation. The moment they enter the door of faith, the task of Christian education begins.

You might consider Christian camping in the light of the raising of Lazarus. The Master issued three commands that remarkable day; two of them to the friends who stood by, and one to the dead man. I see three basic elements of Christian camping in this story in John 11.

Many campers come to us dead in trespasses and sins, to use Paul's phrase from Ephesians 2. They come wearing all manner of shrouds: lust, falsehood, pride; sometimes drugs and disease. These are the trappings of spiritual death. The fact that campers bring problems to camp should not surprise leaders.

Christian campers also come in shrouds, problems lingering from the old nature. Camp would hardly be needed if campers were fully mature. Helping them find cleansing and release is the grand purpose of camp.

Jesus' first command at Lazarus' grave called for action. "Take away the stone!" Opening a grave offends the sensibilities. Death odors are never pleasant. Surely Jesus could shout through a mountain, but He commanded those who stood by to remove the barrier that hindered the dead man from hearing.

Causing people to *hear* the gospel demands more than speaking gospel words. There's hardly a young person in camp who has not seen a Bible verse or heard evangelist on TV, or read "Jesus Saves" on bumper stickers. That's the gospel in its simplest form. But many have never really *heard* that Jesus offers them life.

When you bring people to camp, you find many ways to remove barriers of suspicion, ignorance, prejudice, and fear. You do this by living with campers in a true-to-life atmosphere for an extended time where they can witness the gospel in real people. Many times a day the camper hears the gospel, not in a church setting, which may be alien to his usual life pattern, but in adventure, play, and an array of new experiences. As a counselor, you can roll away gravestones where spiritual death holds young campers.

Jesus' second command was directed to Lazarus, now four days dead. Sometimes we seem to believe that soul-winning is a human task. Not at all! We can only remove barriers through a clear witness, so God can speak to the person. This witness includes the salvation formula, but far more. A person finds life in Christ completely through the work of God. No friend of Lazarus dashed into the tomb to apply artificial respiration. Jesus cried, "Lazarus, come forth!" and he came. The story does not tell us *how* he came out. We are told that he emerged with grave wrappings binding hands, feet, and head. God worked the miracle of new life for a man still wrapped with grave-clothes.

Then Jesus issued His third command. To those who stood by He said, "Loose him and let him go." That's Christian education. Surely this is the ministry of the Christian camp, your ministry as a counselor. Campers will not be perfect, but neither are you. But you are moving toward freedom, toward maturity, toward cleansing. We share the privilege of helping one another escape the shroud.

Helping campers discover freedom in Christ is one aim of the counselor. Christian freedom is both theological and practical, but too often we major in theology, making everyday life seem almost incidental to the gospel. The New Testament teaches that everyday life *is* the gospel; a life of love, joy, peace, patience, kindness, goodness, faithfulness, gentleness, self-control. It is summed up in one word—Christlikeness.

Everyone learns more from seeing than hearing, and camp

offers young people a week-long object lesson in the gospel. You become the object. Don't hide behind that grand Christian alibi, "Don't look at me, look to Jesus!" Unless counselors become Christlike, not much will happen to campers.

GOALS FOR THE CAMP

Considering all the kids in the world, no camp should operate at less than capacity. We have discussed the spiritual purposes of winning campers to Christ and leading them toward spiritual maturity. Let's look at several specific goals which you as a counselor can help achieve. Growth is one.

How big is too big? You can't determine that numerically. As long as the camper enjoys a satisfying experience with spiritual results, total numbers are of little consequence. Given enough land, buildings, and leaders, there seems to be no practical limit to the number that can be served each session.

But having established a practical maximum for your facilities, *attendance* becomes a vital factor. Every empty cot is a lost opportunity, not to mention the difficulties caused for the camp treasurer. Many financial problems can be solved by filling all the cots with campers. A good counselor is the camp's most powerful promotional agent. Campers who have a bad week will not be back, no matter how fetching the promotional movies and brochures might be.

Some camps need to explore new territories for recruiting campers, and every counselor should be a recruiter. One small church set a goal of fifty campers for the next season. When the season approached the quota had not quite been met, the people visited homes in the neighborhood, inviting children to camp. Since most Christian camp fees are less than secular private camps', prospects were not hard to find. The quota was exceeded, and several children from neighborhood homes found Christ. Camp is a prime evangelistic opportunity.

Another church opened its heart to an orphanage in Mexico, sponsoring children even though they spoke only Spanish. When other campers discovered that the orphans had no spending money, they pooled their funds to give each child a dollar. Then the orphans learned that the camp planned to take a missionary offering, and each one tithed his or her spending money. When I talked with the leader, tears filled his eyes. Five of the orphans had found Christ. Reaching more campers means touching more hearts for the Master.

GOALS FOR COUNSELOR

Ask almost any camp director what his or her greatest need is and the reply will be, "Better counselors." Most camps need more money, and many desire more land. Construction never seems to end. But when camping comes down to basic issues, better counseling looms as the greatest need.

Camp counselors make up one of the largest groups of Christian lay workers. The growing number of salaried counselors, particularly head counselors, is a gratifying development. But the majority who serve in camp continue to be volunteers, and most of them serve for a one-week period.

We have pointed out that a camper is exposed to more gospel influence in one week at camp than through regular church attendance the rest of the year. This is no way demeans the church, of which camp is but an extension, but it points out the responsibility assigned to camping in general and to the counselor in particular. The counselor spends more hours with the camper than all other staff members.

The counselor is responsible to many. First you are accountable to God, who has entrusted into your hands for a week or more, a small group of campers. Betraying this trust through carelessness or neglect can result in great harm. You are responsible to pastors and Sunday school teachers, who share your concern for the camper's welfare.

You are responsible to the camp director and sponsors. The investment of many people focuses on your cabin where you determine whether camp succeeds or fails.

And you are responsible to parents, who rely on you to care for their children. Making the rounds one evening, I paused near a cabin where the counselor had stepped out. I heard the boys talking. One or two were building their egos by foul language and stories. Lads sharing this cabin were being exposed to thoughts alien to their parents' desires. The counselor lost an opportunity to send his campers off to sleep with wholesome thoughts in their hearts. Parents trust you to care for their children's minds, bodies, and souls.

The responsibility you should feel will most keenly concern that small group who share the cabin with you. What you are, some of them may become. That's a responsibility! The camper leaves home and family and the distractions of a godless world. Several times each day he or she focuses on spiritual matters; the Bible, prayer, God's claim on each person. Conditions are ideal for the Holy Spirit to work. Yet with all these advantages, you remain camping's greatest force. Young people accept a gospel that works, and camp provides the laboratory where faith can be demonstrated.

Your Personal Goals

While you sharpen camping skills, determine that you will keep on growing as God's person committed to a great task. Many years ago I coached a playground football team, a rugged bunch of athletes who averaged 83 pounds. I recalled from earlier years that football boils down to two fundamentals: blocking and tackling. Since I knew little about the fine points of the game, I concentrated on those fundamentals. My team went undefeated through the season. We won all four games. If you want to be a winner, concentrate on the fundamentals.

The fundamentals for Christian growth are the Bible and prayer. Too often Christians concentrate on trick plays or fancy formations, unaware that those who use these must first master the fundamentals. Until you develop a personal devotional life, you can expect little spiritual strength. That should be your major personal goal.

A PATTERN FOR PERSONAL DEVOTIONS

A place to begin, if you have not found a satisfying pattern, might be to adopt one manageable Scripture portion and live with it for a time. It doesn't matter too much where you begin, for the Lord uses the whole Bible as the textbook for living.

Strive to master the *ideas* of your adopted portion. Read the portion several times a day. Often a key verse or phrase will emerge with special richness.

Having read the portion until its ideas are familiar, discipline yourself to think through the principal ideas at idle moments through the day. You will find the words of your chosen passages forming quiet background music for your thoughts. Remember Psalm 1:2? "In his law he meditates day and night." Writing the Bible passage on a card you can tuck in your purse or pocket will aid you in remembering it.

Two spiritual adventures will become evident as you follow this plan. You will be delighted with the insights you gain into God's Word, small things you missed in beloved passages. And you will be gratified how often your companion passage exactly fits an emergency in your inner life!

Early in this devotional exploration of one passage you will discover a new dimension of prayer. You will find yourself talking the passage back to the Lord, thanking Him for promises, questioning puzzling concepts, claiming provisions for life. You'll find a new basis for prayer that will expand into frequent conversations with God about small things around you. The Bible becomes God's personal message as you respond with your thoughts and feelings.

On the surface this approach might seem too limiting. The Bible is a large book with treasures on every page. Can a Christian afford to linger for days or weeks in one chapter? Indeed he or she can, for such lingering creates a hunger that carries a person beyond that passage, resulting in more Bible reading than ever before!

How long should you remain in one passage? Until you become fully at home in it. You will feel gentle regret at taking up a new passage, like leaving an old friend. But when you do, the adventure begins all over again.

I have found this practice becomes true *personal* devotions, God speaking to me according to my needs day by day. Prayer grows to new richness, freed from the stiff, formal utterances we somehow pick up from hearing public prayers. Frequent chats with the Lord whenever the mind is free from pressing matters sweeten each day.

You will find a time for daily reading that fits your schedule. Any learning program demands discipline, but the blessings from ten minutes in the morning will echo throughout the day and linger in your spirit as sleep overtakes you at night.

Here are a few passages you might consider for in-depth devotions:

1 Corinthians 13	Psalm 37:1-9
Galatians 5:22-25	Joshua 1:1-9
2 Peter 1:3-11	John 15:1-11
Psalm 1	1 John 1:1-9
	Isaiah 40:28-31

PLAN FOR PERSONAL GROWTH

You recognize, of course, that counseling demands spiritual maturity. Only as you grow in your Christian life will you improve as a counselor. Camp brings the whole year into focus in one week of ministry, and all the preparation in the world won't help much if you reach camp a spiritually impoverished, defeated Christian. But growth in knowledge is vital too.

Aim at increasing your understanding of campers. Read Christian education books, attend workshops where you can learn from others, participate in church leadership where you can observe young people. Watch for magazine articles dealing with youth and their problems. Many problems counselors suffer grow out of a failure to understand the nature and limitations of the age group they serve.

Build a personal counselor's file. Clip stories and ideas you can use next summer. Swap ideas with other counselors. Read books on camping, jotting down usable ideas. Preserve your evaluation of each year's experience—ideas that worked and that didn't. Become the most proficient counselor you can.

THE CALL TO EXCELLENCE

We have pointed out that evangelism is only the beginning. Winning people to Christ is not enough, if by "winning" we settle for a momentary decision. Saving faith always leads to action, a lifelong search for the high purpose to which Christ calls His followers. Your aims for the camper include the challenge to excellence in all of life, as befits a person who belongs to God.

EXCELLENCE IN FAITH

Sometimes Christian youth are accused of being shallow. If this is true, guilt must be shared by leaders who fail to recognize that young people respond to challenging leadership. As a counselor you must exhibit and teach the high standard of faith Paul wrote to Timothy: "Be thou an example of the believers." Lead your campers toward excellence through meaningful devotions and conversation. Acquaint them with Christ's deeper claims to full commitment, but don't expect young Christians to run before they have learned to walk!

EXCELLENCE IN VOCATION

Challenge campers to adventure in vocation. Countless Christian leaders have heard God's call while in camp. God still seeks people with willing hearts for missionary posts around the world. But avoid creating tension between those committed to church-related vocations and those who are not. God's call to any job is equally valid. Urge campers toward occupations where they can serve people. Help campers discover the worth of their persons, and challenge them to become their best, wherever God may place them.

EXCELLENCE IN SERVICE

Urge campers to enlist immediately in God's service in the church, at school, or through outreach ministries. Churches have sometimes been reluctant to use young people. The theory that teenagers can't effectively teach Sunday school has been exploded. Older youths can work with younger children in club programs. Remind campers that service includes the family. Many Christian young people become careless at home, reflecting ingratitude for the sacrifices parents make. Youth gladly enter the serious work of God's kingdom when they are challenged.

EXCELLENCE IN LEADERSHIP

The counselor who succeeds best is the one who does the least. Can this be true? Yes, if you work at developing leadership among campers. More skill is required to work through your campers than to do a task yourself. Depending on the campers' age, utilize every opportunity to cultivate leadership skills. This doesn't suggest self-determination for immature campers, but you will find opportunities for sharing leadership. When decision-making or planning needs arise, consider how your campers can share. Use them to plan devotions and outings. Skill in leadership comes through practice under guidance. Show campers how to lead, and don't do for them what they are capable of doing, even when their performance can't match yours.

So this is the heart of the matter, focusing on our goals as servants of Christ through camping. Throughout history Christian movements have degenerated into mere institutions, impressive and enduring, but no longer soul-winning, life-changing forces. Camping can lose its spiritual verve too.

While we must never sacrifice excellence in facility or program through indifference to quality, we must constantly call ourselves back to the established goal: to fulfill God's purpose in the lives of people.

9

Decisions, Decisions

Christian camping can be viewed from two perspectives. Some see camp as a place where young people come to gain whatever values and experiences they desire, sort of a *buffet* approach. Camp offers a variety of religious and recreational options. The camper chooses according to his or her inclinations.

Others see camp as a dynamic part of the Christian cause, with sharply defined objectives. The primary objective seeks to lead campers into positive, lasting choices. Admittedly and unashamedly, the camp seeks to lead campers into crisis experiences calling for decisions. The trouble is, many camps like this began to measure their success by the numbers of such decisions recorded each season.

The problem is quite obvious, for the meaning of a "decision" cannot be determined at the close of a week or a summer. Only decisions that change the life of the camper have lasting significance. Yet the urgency to record a successful season exerts a subtle pressure to make sure decisions were registered.

We have already considered the counselor's role in guiding campers toward decisions that lead to spiritual growth. But the subject is so important that we will probe deeper. The fact is, every camper in your cabin group will make significant decisions. Impossible? No, inevitable. The decisions may not be the hand-raising or go-forward kind, but decisions will be made. Furthermore, the camper will bring to camp a whole collection of previously made decisions. Your task will be to help the camper organize these many streams of influence into a life-changing force.

There's a girl in New England who made a decision one night. She was the only youngster in the small group that turned out for a Thursday night missionary rally. Carol was perhaps ten years old, shy and pretty. We talked about her school, her daddy's job, a new baby brother, just trivia. Carol took the chair next to mine as we formed a circle. We shared a hymnbook.

In the course of my talk on personal involvement in Christ's mission I turned to Carol and said, "Do you know, there never was a girl exactly like you before in the whole world?"

She dropped her eyes and smiled shyly as the group focused on her. "Furthermore," I continued, "There will never again be a girl just like you. I think the Lord has a special work for you."

I'll never forget the moment that followed, though perhaps no one else in the room sensed anything. Carol lifted her eyes and held mine. Probably she had never thought of herself just this way. (Who knows how a little girl thinks? Or what influences God brings into a life as He leads a child toward His purpose?) The depth of awareness on this little black girl's face lingers with me. I think she decided, at that moment to be God's special person.

But was that a "decision?" She didn't raise her hand, go forward or give testimony. Can you count one fleeting response as a decision? Well, I gave up counting quite a while ago, though you may keep whatever records you find necessary. This was one of the small decisions, that blends with many more to bring about a discovery of God's grand purpose, the kind of decision some of your campers may make next summer.

Decision Dropouts

Great harm has been done to campers through careless handling of decisions. Shallow decisions draw deserved criticism.

Some people challenge the validity of camp statistics. One study revealed that 100 pledges to missionary services were reported for every worker who actually reached the field. What happened to the 99?

No doubt many decision dropouts were sincere enough, but the invitation proved so general and the issues of responding so obscure or trivial that the campers could do no more than indicate genuine interest. At other times, young people are led to declare a purpose they cannot fulfill, for all the facts are not made clear.

Some missionaries tell of encounters in youth where God pointed out a specific work in a definite field. But more commonly, it's a series of struggles and nudgings that ultimtely lead to a work they had scarcely dreamed of. A decision is a point of beginning. Only those decisions where God is at work possess spiritual significance.

Your task as a counselor is to help campers understand how God guides, and lead them to weigh carefully the responsibilities that follow public decisions. When this happens, fewer decisions may be recorded, but the dropout percentage will decline.

Many decision dropouts result from the absence of follow-up. Even a spark of concern must be nourished. Be ready to help the camper follow through, for decisions that demand nothing are cheaply made.

AVOIDING EMPTY DECISIONS

Decisions statistics can mean almost anything. Campers come to some camps expecting calls for decisions. It's part of camp tradition. They understand the expected responses. Hands raised, campers going forward, decision cards to sign. It's all part of camp. Furthermore, making a decision gains favorable notice from the staff. Prayers are heard in behalf of those who have not yet made a decision. Under such conditions empty decisions become almost inevitable.

Some leaders have overeacted against empty decisions, eliminating public invitations completely. Others grow testy at any questioning of invitations. Still others carelessly make decisions the object of humor. However you look at it, you must guard against shallow, falsely-motivated decisions, for spiritual progress remains the product of life's decisions.

Planning for meaningful decisions requires that you consider several factors. The ages and backgrounds of your campers should influence your planning. The nature of your camp's program should also influence how decisions will be encouraged. The experience and abilities of staff people is another factor. A most significant consideration grows out of your camp's objectives, and your insight into the nature of "decisions."

A group of alarmed camp leaders met to discuss an apparent trend away from evangelism in camp. Statistics revealed a decline in the number of "salvation" decisions. Then one of the group produced another statistic. Conversions had increased significantly in other agencies serving the camp constituency; the boys and girls clubs, Sunday School, Vacation Bible School. They concluded that a greater percentage of their campers were already Christians when they came to camp.

Continuing the same emphasis on salvation decisions under those circumstances made little more sense than requiring competent swimmers to remain in the beginners' class. The need obviously called for a new approach, while remaining alert to campers who had not yet received Christ as Lord and Saviour.

Pressure-type evangelism among little children is unwise. But ignoring the need for conversion among young campers is more unwise. Recognize both the needs and limitations of each age-group. To begin with, you must help campers discover where they are spiritually.

Occasionally—with no intention to generate an artificial emotional climate—a high moment of spiritual awareness steals over a group. At such times care must be exercised to identify the gentle work of the Holy Spirit and the response of the human spirit.

One August morning Western Union delivered a telegram. The sender was one of my parishioners, a Bible camp enthusiast. The wire declared that revival had broken out at camp with scores making decisions.

Having never observed a revival, I drove 150 miles to take a look. I found the camp in near chaos! Campers were sullen and staff members were grim. My parishioner had fired off his telegram an hour too soon. That must be the shortest revival on record.

What happened? A campfire consecration service brought scores of campers forward to confess sin and pledge themselves for missions, witnessing, renewal—all kinds of spiritual commitments. A spirit of love and joy overflowed as minutes passed, then hours. Staff members joined the campers in confession and commitment.

But adults grow tired sooner than campers, and finally the director blew his whistle. But the campers' bouyant spirits could not be turned off by a whistle! Playful, spontaneous games of hide-and-seek began between campers and staff, soon degenerated into scolding, then threats. The "revival" was over.

The number making decisions at the campfire probably set an all-time high for that camp. No doubt it was an enriching experience, and the participants had no intention to deceive. They acted sincerely under the spell of the moment, but an hour or so later, they found life just as it was before, with the same adult/youth tensions and the same real-life conflict.

The campfire decisions and confessions were valid at the moment, but they proved to be empty in the ensuing hours. We must not discount the worth of such experiences, yet we see the need for discernment into the subtleties of the campers' perception of spiritual responsibility.

Planning for Decisions

Whatever cautions we must observe, the high purpose of Christian camping is served when we encourage campers to make decisions for Christ. The place to begin is with the salvation decision. Either a camper has trusted Christ for salvation or has not. There can be no middle ground.

CALL TO SALVATION

Early in your camp session you will want to help campers discover for themselves where they stand with Jesus Christ. Have they exercised faith to personally receive God's gift? It is important that the camper know. Open conversation can help campers discover where they are.

Beware of telling a camper he surely *must* be a Christian because of some past experience or favorable circumstances. You'll find many *cultural* Christians and *hereditary* Christians sitting comfortably in your cabin groups. They need to be born again!

Beware too of discouraging weak Christians by declaring, "A real Christian could never do *that!*" You need only look within to discover that real Christians can do *that*, and much more. The fact that a camper cares about failures provides hope of spiritual light.

Somehow, through personal conversation or group sharing, discover how each camper sees him or herself in relation to Christ. Beyond conversion they will find a spiritual pathway with valleys and peaks. You know about this, for you walk that trail too. Some campers come with a deep gorge to cross. This may be their crisis decision.

Bear in mind that the theft of a dime may weigh as heavily on the heart of a junior as the embezzlement of a million on a banker's. Never treat a camper's burden lightly. Challenge your campers to face the known issues in their lives, and seek God's grace for growth.

CALL TO RENEWAL

In Chapter Six we reviewed the various kinds of needs that lead to camper decisions. All Christians sense the need for spiritual renewal now and then, and the atmosphere of the Christian camp should stir the heart. Most campers are exposed to more Bible teaching at camp than they experience throughout the rest of the year. Jesus said, "Now ye are clean through the word which I have spoken unto you" (John 15:3). Opportunity should be given for campers to seek renewal as the Scriptures reveal needs. This is a precious opportunity to be conveted by the counselor.

CALL TO VOCATION

As campers mature, the call to vocation must be considered. Walk carefully here! God's appointment never places one Christian in some spiritually favored spot, while another is simply dropped off any old place. Certain callings have been glamorized, and many a miserable missionary has languished in a foreign land, a tribute to Grandma's ego.

Yet God does call young Christians to church-related vocations. Camp has been the place of decision for a great many missionaries, pastors, and other Christian leaders. And most of them confess they found help through a camp leader, maybe one like you.

TIMES FOR DECISIONS

In addition to an awareness of the several kinds of decisions campers may make, your plan must include *times* for decisions. I will discuss later the *teachable moment.* You should plan to be alert for signs that such a moment has come. This involves little more than maintaining an available spirit and a sensitivity to your campers' moods. Yet specific programing for decisions is essential too.

The invitation after chapel provides a valuable decision-making opportunity. With all its problems, the public invitation still accounts for many real decisions. Here is the counselor's open door, for the camper identifies some need by responding. The method for helping him or her toward a decision remains much the same as that which you use in other settings. Chapel, campfires, and devotional programs may conclude with an invitation for decision-making. Personal counsel is vital.

Your plan for decisions should include a personal interview with each camper in your cabin group. This may be structured or casual, but don't let the camp period slip by without some opportunity to chat privately with each camper.

Telling your campers that you plan to interview each one opens the way. Probably you will be required to write a camper report. An interview to gather information for that report can expand into other areas. The problem with the scheduled interview is obvious. Campers tend to respond with answers they feel you want to hear, and with information they wish to appear on the report that goes home.

The teachable moment concept offers the strongest setting for your interview. You risk not being present when this moment arises, but as the Holy Spirit leads and other factors necessary for the camper to face his real needs are present, you are likely to guide your campers to lasting decisions.

YOU AND THE CAMPER'S DECISION

In addition to planning to meet various needs, and determining to chat with each camper, there remains the matter of how your campers view you. In one camp of my boyhood we called our counselor "The Warden." I'm sure we used the term kindly, for I remember him as a fine man. But some counselors see themselves largely as wardens, with inmates living always on the edge of rebellion.

Other counselors see themselves as big brother or sister. Worse, they seek to be the camper's buddy. A few suffer the Napoleon complex, and they are sure losers!

Life will offer you few opportunities so potentially rich as the counselor-camper relationship. If you can become a trusted friend, you can't find a more helpful relationship.

A friend is one who will listen and not tell, one who doesn't reject you no matter what you reveal. One who hurts with you and laughs with you.

Being a camper's friend demands honesty and integrity, plus more humility than most of us possess. The measure of your friendship is your capacity to listen while the camper examines his problems by talking about them, and listening takes time. Plan for time to be a loving, helpful listener.

THE TEACHABLE MOMENT

How can you help campers make lasting decisions? This requires wisdom and humility. Ultimately, life-changing decisions must be the work of God. We will look at several ways to help campers reach the point of personal commitment, but you must guard against confining yourself to a rigid formula. God's Spirit may use a formula, then again, it's entirely possible that He may not.

Some educators make much of what they call the "teachable moment." They explain that this moment cannot be scheduled. A person learns when proper conditions are met, and certain needs are fulfilled in the learner. This fits the camp experience, for decision-making is partly an educational matter. Based on understanding and motivation, the camper responds.

One factor beyond your control is the camper's *heart*-response. No formula can determine this. Since the response can come at any time, often at unlikely times, your task is to be ready.

Several years ago I was paddling down the Allegash in northern Maine with a youngster in the bow of the canoe. He was about 12, from a troubled home, and barely able to read. But how he could talk! He chattered incessantly until I wanted to throttle him.

We were hopelessly behind the other canoes. The river was boulder-strewn and I'd yell "Right!" or "Left!" The lad could never decide which was his left or right hand before we collided with a boulder. I understood why the boys refused to paddle with him. A canoe trip simply wasn't the place for a kid like this, I grumbled, pitying myself.

Then silence. The river flowed quietly, no rapids or threatening boulders. The boy spoke, "Cap, were you ever scared?"

"Sure," I replied. "Lots of times."

"I mean *really* scared, like maybe you would die?"

"I guess so," I said.

"That's how I felt back there," he said.

I scanned the last few hours. I could recall nothing to frighten a boy. "What scared you?" I asked.

"When you asked us to tell about God." he replied.

At noon we had paused on a sand bar for lunch and devotions, a group of about 20 men and boys. We read the Word, and I invited the boys to tell how they came to know Christ. A few responded with routine testimonies. We prayed together, picked up our luncheon litter, and paddled away, my partner and I bringing up the rear. Certainly nothing terrifying had occurred.

"I know God," the lad continued. "I accepted Jesus after church one night. I wanted to tell the guys but I got so scared and my heart pounded . . . I couldn't talk. They laugh at me anyhow. I got a Bible, but I can't read good . . ."

He was still for a while and so was I. I wanted to tell him how sorry I was for my selfish thoughts, for forgetting that every boy is important, even though he can't read well or keep up with the others.

We enjoyed several talks about God's ways in the days that remained of our trip, sandwiched in between his chattering and my futile yelling of navigational orders. Maybe I helped him understand some things about God's Word and about himself. He taught me a few things too. The teachable moment works both ways!

You—A Living Letter

God will work through you as you live out your personal Christian commitment before your campers. Camp counseling is neither difficult nor mysterious. You don't need a major in psychology. You need only be yourself and bring to camp what skills you can muster, bathed in the joy of living and the wonder of serving Christ. You are God's message, a living letter of truth. An awesome thought to ponder.

Invitations in chapel and around campfires continue to attract many genuine camper responses, but you should see these as the climax of many smaller decisions, perhaps reaching back into early childhood. What a camper understands will follow after a decision is most important. Your life should provide a pattern for him.

The attitude you bring to camp will determine your success in helping campers reach life-changing decisions. Everyone hungers for acceptance. You can't turn attitudes on and off at will. If you genuinely love your campers and open your heart to them with acceptance, decisions may come at any time.

You'll find some campers more lovable than others. When you meet a camper you dislike, examine yourself. You may discover that you need to do some spiritual homework. The camper you dislike often has deep spiritual needs. You can work out your problems together!

The Twelve held a conference one day as they walked through Galilee. Perhaps they walked in a grim knot, their voices low. Their subject: Who was the greatest among them?

Imagine their embarrassment when Jesus said, "What were you discussing on the way?" Of course He already knew. But so often Jesus taught by calling for a confession.

The truth Jesus left with those followers must become clear to you if your ministry to campers is to count.

"If any man desire to be first, the same shall be last of all, and servant of all. And he took a child, and set him in the midst of them: and when he had taken him in his arms, he said unto them, Whosoever shall receive one of such children in my name, receiveth me (Mark 9:35-37).

Jesus taught that greatness is serving, and He used a child for His example. Jesus' words should speak to you. I think about them when I remember a boy asking, "Cap, were you ever scared? *Really* scared?"

CAMPER HELPING CAMPER

I visited a missionary one wintry March weekend, and he hauled me by snowmobile 25 miles through the Canadian wilderness to an isolated village. We shared a wonderful evening with some Chippewa kids in a schoolhouse, singing and telling stories.

The next morning as we finished breakfast in the missionary's cabin he said, "I'll show you something." Scraping the remains of our breakfast into a frying pan, he opened the door and dropped the scraps on the snow. Then he banged the pan with a spatula.

Dogs came running from everywhere! All colors, sizes and

unrecognizable breeds. They came yelping and barking, all except one. He just loped casually toward the cabin. The missionary said, "Now watch."

One growl sent the other dogs backward. The boss dog gulped the table scraps, pausing now and then to snarl at an intruder who inched too close. When the food was about gone, the boss dog trotted off and the others moved in. The dogs of that village were very well organized!

THE BOSS CAMPER

You discover the same phenomenon when you attempt to mix two herds of horses, or eight or ten campers! Subconsciously the group begins to build that mysterious hierarchy via small battles, mostly verbal. You must deal with this basic fact of nature-animal and human. Leadership *will* assert itself. The right kind of camper leadership can significantly affect decisions.

CABIN SPIRIT AND DECISIONS

How you form your cabin group will greatly influence your efforts to help campers toward lasting decisions. The impact of friend on friend probably equals your personal influence. The peer group is a force to be reckoned with. If you find a rebellious boss camper, you're in for trouble.

A loyal, spiritually sensitive leader among the campers will be anxious to help other campers, and will be a benediction to you. This calls for careful, wise leadership on your part. You cannot impose one camper's leadership over others. Nor can you command camper loyalty to yourself. How campers relate to one another and to you is a matter for much concern and much prayer.

The brief periods most camps offer hardly permit in-depth acquaintance, let alone the kind of patient work required to change poor attitudes formed over long periods of time in unhappy homes. At best, you can show campers what Christ means to you as you live among them. Most campers respond to sincere friendship, even the rebels.

Since you are aware that your cabin group will engage in

the tussle to see who's boss, and that campers will exert at least as much influence on each other as you, watch for every opportunity to build a warm group spirit. Discussion times offer some help.

DISCUSSION AND GROWTH

Many counselors despair of discussion because campers refuse to focus on the assigned devotional topic. We think a successful discussion occurs only when campers are responding with the answers found in a study guide. But some campers probably haven't the slightest interest in your study guide!

What does capture their interest? Find out, and talk about it, even though the topic is nondevotional. Once your campers feel comfortable, you are moving toward the condition required for a worthwhile "discussion."

On one occasion a counselor sensed strong questionings among her campers. Most of them professing Christians. They knew the right answers, but something was wrong. The wise counselor announced that for evening devotions they would conduct a "doubt fest." Every camper was invited to write down her favorite doubt, or several, if she wished.

Discussion was no problem in that cabin! Some girls obviously tried to shock the counselor, who refused to be shocked. Others repeated age-old problems. Others revealed deep, troubled thoughts. The campers learned that others shared their doubts, even the counselor! They found that a doubting Christian can talk over doubts with God, and search the Scriptures for answers. Doubting was no longer unmentionable.

Much more good was accomplished for that group of girls by discussing doubts than if the counselor had opened her devotional guide and plowed through the night's exercise, asking routine questions and collecting pat answers. More Scripture was explored searching for answers to real questions than the group would have absorbed through a formal lesson.

Perhaps the difference can be summed up in two words: *instruction* and *discovery*. Proper instruction includes discovery, but too often camp teaching, intended to bring about decisions, results in little more than reciting a lesson in the general direction of the campers, with campers' minds wander to their felt needs.

Whatever devotional guides you receive, absorb them so thoroughly that you can wander from the outline when campers give evidence of interest in one area. When they begin reacting to an idea, progress toward a useful discussion is under way.

As the camp period progresses, you should find ways to build concern for each other among your campers. Occasionally an eager-beaver camper creates ill will by pestering another camper about a spiritual matter. Almost as distracting is the adult who comes to camp toting a monstrous Bible and overwhelming zeal. He or she corners campers at random with aggressive questions about their spiritual state. Hyperactive glands are no substitute for the Holy Spirit!

Your task as one who would help campers toward life-changing decisions calls for care in developing the spirit of the cabin group so that campers help one another. This requires quiet devotional times as well as free-wheeling discussions. One approach to effective group worship is to cultivate the campers' devotions, teaching them the nature of worship.

DEVOTIONS AND DECISIONS

I recall a scene of beauty in a Wisconsin high school camp. The setting was picturesque with towering pines and rustic buildings, trimmed in deep red. The camp tradition called for a personal quiet time just before vespers. Scattered throughout the camp, I saw the campers here and there, Bibles open, quietly reading. Nearly one hundred campers, and not a sound except the sounds of forest, meadow, and lake in the evening. These campers were discovering worship.

Your camp may not offer this tradition, but you can suggest a quiet time for your campers. This might provide a profitable use of the quiet period after lunch.

I advocate as widely as possible a concentrated reflection on a limited number of Scriptures, rather than the random study of many passages so common in camps. Personal meditation on the same passages you will use for cabin devotions later in the evening brings double enrichment. And if you had the good fortune to explore that same passage in the morning Bible class, so much the better!

As your cabin group experiences a growing love for one another, and trust develops between you and the campers, the climate is right for decisions. Some will be made in the group as you talk and pray. Others will be made in private, with only God's Spirit the witness. Often a camper will open his heart, and you will help him or her choose God's way to saving faith, renewal, victory over a problem, or commitment to God's life-calling. Decisions flow easily when trusted friends are near.

Building friendships with each camper presents a great challenge. Helping campers build helpful friendships with one another is an equal challenge.

Decisions through Discovery

We have considered the critics of camp decisions who point to the dropouts. Probably we've all stood around the campfire and listened to repetitions of failure to fulfill last year's pledge, but *this* year . . . You're reasonably sure the same campers will repeat their vows next summer.

We discussed the danger of empty decisions. I would not imply that campers deliberately make empty decisions. Often they haven't thought the issue through, they merely respond-ed to the level of the group's motivation.

SOURCES OF DECISIONS

A decision resulting from stirred emotions will pass when the mood changes. This struck sorrow to my heart as a young Christian. The buoyancy I felt in the evening camp service led me to make all manner of promises to God and man. But the next morning I felt low. I wondered if I really was a Christian.

By and by I learned that feeling low is my normal state in the morning, and that buoyancy often is my normal state in the evening. I am what armchair psychologists call an Owl. Some people are Larks, morning people. Many young owls wake up disappointed.

Some decisions might be incurred through logic. A forceful, statistic-laden purveyor of truth overwhelms the mind. What he says must be so! But along comes another powerful mind, perhaps a respected school teacher, and logic wavers. Many keen minds reject the Bible. Decisions based on logic can often be toppled by logic.

Then there's the decision forged by the peer group, a nearly irresistible pressure. It's true that God can use the influence of friends to lead to genuine decisions, but such decisions can be sheer sociology. When the camper returns home to friends who are not Christians, this kind of decision is forgotten.

Sometimes a decision is wrought by intimidation. I have doubts about the stories of a zealot who strongarmed a timid soul into the Kingdom by threatening bodily harm if the poor fellow didn't love Jesus. But other kinds of intimidation exist. Young campers sometimes fall prey to this. Wishing to please a hero leader, they agree to almost anything.

One of God's special servants to children, Wally Zwemke, has developed a good approach to helping youngsters who respond to invitations. After dismissing the group he invites those who wish to receive Christ as Saviour to return. He asks each one to talk with him personally before being assigned to a counselor.

Wally asks one question: Why did you come? If the answer isn't clear, he lovingly sends the youngster on his way to return the following day. When the response reveals an understanding or sincere concern, a counselor leads the child through the Scriptures.

Decisions caused by gentle coercion, or hero worship, or love for a leader, can be destroyed by the next hero or love. Which decisions are real, then? Only those that God achieves through His Word.

THE BIBLE AND DECISIONS

One of my college professors defined teaching as that process whereby information passes from the instructor's notebook to the student's notebook without going through the mind of either. Do we find some camp teaching like this?

Since decisions are the work of God based on His Word, it follows that camp Bible study is essential to decision-making. How can we get God's Word beyond the camper's notebook and into his heart? You have learned that I like the word *discovery.*

An old man walked a wooded trail, his grandsons close behind. They did not observe him reach into his pocket and remove something: When they reached a high point where the view was grand, the old man begged to rest. While the boys played he tossed the object from his pocket to an open spot on the trail, a nearly perfect arrowhead from a long-gone day. It blended with the rocks and dust of the pathway.

At last the old man called, "Come boys, see how many different *stones* you can find." The boys scurried about, searching.

Then there was a cry, "Grandpa! Grandpa! Look what I've found!"

I confess that's one of those true-to-life-stories that becomes quoted as fact, but the principle is worthy. What a delight, while teaching to see an old truth capture a person's mind for the first time. Much of our teaching says too much, leaving nothing for the mind of the hearer to discover.

A high school senior rushed into the classroom one Sunday with her Bible open, her face aglow. Only recently she had met God on a camp-out with the youth group.

"Look!" she said. "Look what I've found!" Her finger traced a simple verse. *And you are complete in Him.* Tears of joy glistened in her eyes.

I don't know what struggles she had passed through, but in God's Word she found the answer and accepted God's peace. She *discovered* a treasure, and it became hers for all time.

If camp decisions are to be lasting, they must be based on God's Word. But what about the camper who refuses to accept the Scriptures? That's a hard question. Perhaps the most difficult truth a Christian leader must acknowledge is his or her helplessness in the face of unbelief.

In another chapter we will examine a camp Bible study plan that has been used in many camps to implant biblical truth in campers' hearts. The plan focuses on one brief Bible passage and one key verse each day, returning to it three times, morning, noon, and night. I learned the value of this plan on a rugged mountain in Maine one August day.

I shared with a group of men and boys as they tackled Baxter Peak on Mt. Katahdin—the highest point in the state. As we neared the summit, a storm swept in. Hikers disappeared in the cloudy mists. A boulder loomed in my face as I walked. We were forced to abandon the climb and seek a trail down the mountain.

As we moved below the clouds, vision again became comfortable, and nothing remained but the careful, sometimes risky descent.

Throughout the trip we had lived in John 15, dwelling particularly on verse 7. Some might say our Bible content that trip was too meager, just 12 or 15 verses for the whole week, and only one memory verse! We didn't even bother to memorize that, we just repeated it several times a day. And each evening around the campfire we'd ask, "Anything good to tell about today?"

This night, bone tired from the day's climb, we huddled around the fire for brief devotions before seeking our bedrolls. "Anything good to report?"

Our smallest camper spoke. "That verse we've been saying—I didn't really know much what it meant until today. I asked the Lord to get me off that mountain! I didn't think I could make it. But I did!"

We spoke the verse once again around the fire: "If you abide in Me, and My words abide in you, you shall ask what you will, and it shall be done unto you." One boy found out that God's truth works, even on a stormy mountain. That's worth knowing.

These stories are to impress on you one truth: decisions must be founded on Scripture. Maybe not always on one verse, but surely on the principles found in the Bible.

You will learn that God always works through His Word.

Your task is to lead campers into his treasure field where they can pick up nuggets here and there. But don't wander too far! Find a rich lode and pause there.

DECISIONS THROUGH CONVERSATION

Somewhere I lost one of my favorite photos. You recall Uncle John Libke, mentioned in Chapter One. The photo showed this aging man seated with a boy on a woodpile at Center Lake Camp in Michigan. The boy had just accepted Uncle John's invitation. I quietly followed to observe.

Uncle John's invitation for children was simple. He'd complete his Bible story, then invite all the boys and girls who wanted to talk about trusting Jesus as Saviour to follow him. He'd step down off the platform and walk outdoors.

On this occasion one boy responded. I captured a rare picture. The boy was totally engrossed in Uncle John's words. His Bible open on a log, the old man explained the way of salvation and heard the lad's prayer of faith.

THE GREATEST PRIVILEGE

Often in your counseling ministry you will find opportunity to lead campers to Christ. This is the utimate joy, one you should covet. You may use your own or someone else's method for presenting the Saviour. But be sure to base the seeker's faith on God's promises. Use a few Bible passages, perhaps only one. It is enough that the camper simply receive God's Son as his Lord and Saviour.

I frequently turn to John 1:12. If I must engage in persuasion or argument, I do so with great care, wondering if the camper has been prepared by the Spirit. For unless God is at work, any decision that is reached has little value.

When a camper confesses a positive faith in Christ in prayer, I add my prayer of gratitude for God's gift, then spend a brief time on verses of assurance, basing the campers confidence on God's promise. Then I try to get the camper to tell several people of his or her decision. A confession of faith to one person is as helpful as a public testimony before a crowd.

There's something powerful about a simple conversation, when Jesus is the topic.

BE WORTH TALKING TO

When you gain a camper's confidence so that he or she will open the heart, you have cause to thank the Lord. This is no small victory! Such an achievement grows out of the total camp experience. One careless moment or thoughtless act can destroy confidence and any chance for the trust essential to conversation which leads to decisions.

The challenge before you is to *be worth talking to.* As you evaluate your choicest friendship, ask, why you are attracted to that person? Usually you will discover a quality in conversation that stimulates you. But more often, you find that your close friend is one who lets you talk while he or she listens!

In Chapter Six I suggested that the anatomy of a good camp counselor includes two organs: the heart and the ear, loving and listening. 1 Thessalonians 4:11 contains excellent advice to every camp counselor: "Study to be quiet . . ." One Christian leader placed this text on his desk facing his visitors. What they couldn't see was his private prayer printed on the back: "Lord help me to keep my big mouth shut!"

Most of the problems campers share have a ready solution, and the camper knows what it is. His problem lies in his inability to apply the solution! The liar needs no one to tell him, "Quit lying." He wrestles with a deeper weakness that prompts him to lie.

WAIT FOR THE REAL PROBLEM

As we have mentioned earlier, deep problems usually lie hidden beneath trivia. You must listen long enough to get at the real burden. You won't find too many opportunities to wrestle with the deepest problems because camp allows so few days. But you can be certain you'll fail if you jump on the first sin your camper mentions and start pontificating.

The camper will seek an escape by mentioning some simple matter, almost hoping you will propose an aspirin-like remedy to relieve the pain and forestall facing the real issues. Being honest is one of life's most painful experiences.

A camper will probe and spar to determine at what point you reject him. We mentioned acceptance and love as the foundational qualities for those who would help campers toward life-changing decisions. Sadly, we have been conditioned to react to certain kinds of sin with visible loathing, perhaps to demonstrate our personal piety.

You may hear a sordid story, for these are overwhelming days. But your memory will be adequate to break down the rejection you are conditioned to erect. You know about sin! Without condoning, you listen, for your ear and heart can help work healing.

Often the very act of confession brings healing. God forgives all sin immediately upon confession to Him. It's as easy for God to forgive big sins as little ones.

Turn to the Word for God's answer to sin. 1 John 1:9 lifts the burden. As you pray together, you will be mutually grateful for a loving, forgiving Father. And of course you leave the camper no dread that his story will be repeated.

LET THE CAMPER DECIDE

Not all conversations deal with troublesome sin. Some campers are seeking direction and they need help. A comment usually to be avoided is, "I'll tell you what you ought to do." A better approach is, "What do you think you ought to do?"

A decision belongs to the one who makes it. When you decide, the camper may accept your advice, but it was your decision. Help the camper weigh the options. If your opinion is sought, you may give it.

Often you'll be asked, "How can I know God's leading?" Proverbs 3:5,6 provide an excellent *foundation* for discovering God's way, but the camper must decide which job to take next week, or which school to select in September.

The answer I find most useful is this: Ask God to guide your thinking, then pick the direction that seems best, considering all the circumstances, and start moving. It's sort of like driving a car—it's easier to steer when it's in motion.

Occasionally you may be called on to arbitrate a difference

between campers. Perhaps a camper has wronged another and feels guilty. The best solution to a private problem is a private settlement. A confession need reach no farther than its circle of hurt. Again, allow the offender to make the decision. Forced confessions are generally useless.

Cherish most that conversation when the camper asks, "Can I talk with you a minute?" And he does all the talking! He shares his dreams and fears, his longings for the better life with God, his memories and ambitions, or just life's trivia.

When a young person decides to talk, he's already made an important decision. He's decided you are his friend, and every camper needs a friend with whom he can openly share his dreams. This quality of friendship is rare, and for lack of it, many young Christians fall.

Nurture Those Decisions

Two decisions approximately one year apart changed the course of my life. Both were real. I made one with help, the other alone. At the age of 13, kneeling before a crude plank altar with a friend, I decided for Christ. Many small decisions and not a few deceptions preceded that acceptance of God's gift. But I responded as I knew I must someday, and I gained eternal life.

The second decision found me at another altar—the traditional place for deciding things in that wonderful camp—yielding my life to God for ministry. I was, to say the least, an unlikely candidate.

Perhaps that's why the tired Methodist minister standing before me in his nightshirt in the dormitory said with such a sour countenance, "The ministry? Son, be sure. Be very sure." That was hardly the counsel I sought, but it was good counsel. Since the decision was mine, I was sure.

DECISIONS TAKE TIME

How can we be sure a decision is sincere? Only by giving it time. Don't expect too much too soon from youthful decisions, for growth comes slowly.

I am not suggesting that decisions are unreliable, just that they must be nurtured.

The most sincere, God-inspired decision requires help, and that is no affront to God's sufficiency. To start with, every decision should find verbal expression as soon as possible. A testimony of a decision, removed from its emotional setting, will do much to impress the meaning of the act on the camper. But more remains to be done.

DECISIONS NEED FRIENDS

Christians need friends as they grow. That's the reason for the church. A newly-converted camper sent home to an alien world has little chance for growth. In every instance, a camper who makes a decision must be given friends who will stand by him or her.

Friends from camp form the first line of defense. But camp ends so quickly! Blessed is the camper who came with a cluster of helpful friends at home. The lone camper from a home deserves most careful attention. Perhaps you, the counselor, must give that care, even at considerable effort.

See to it that someone who knows the Lord will offer campers Christian fellowship after camp. Not every young person can break household tradition and become involved in a church. Christians must seek out and sustain this kind of person, understanding the need for wisdom in relating to parents who are not Christians.

We will discuss follow-up detail in Chapter Eleven, but let us recognize that any serious intent to lead campers into life-changing decisions must include some plan for continued growth. Jesus climaxed His great commission by saying, "Teaching them to observe (put into practice) all things whatsoever I have commanded you" (Matthew 28:20). Just leading campers to Christ is not enough.

FOUNDATIONS FOR SURVIVAL

Christian friends are vital, and the church is responsible to care for young people. But ultimately each Christian must learn to walk personally with the Lord. Help campers begin the disciplines of godliness—personal Bible study, prayer, and witness. Encourage them to share actively in church life, to find a church home if they have not had one.

Teach your campers how to study the Bible, how to pray. Pray with each camper before he or she goes home if at all possible. Assure each one that you will continue to pray for him or her.

A big order? Yes. But when you consider the possibilities, the effort required is well spent. A decision is but a beginning, and we all need help.

10

Cabin Bible Study

"A camp setting is the greatest environment for learning today." These were the words of Dr. Ted Ward, university professor, international educational consultant for the Carnegie Foundation, and outstanding Christian communicator, as he addressed hundreds of camp leaders gathered for the international convention of Christian Camping International in Green Lake, Wisconsin.

Dr. Ward went on to explain why his observation was true, and in so doing, he confirmed what camp leaders have known for generations. You can't beat camp as a center for learning!

But does the typical Christian camp take full advantage of this opportunity? More and more camp leaders are discovering a missing dimension to their teaching ministry, and this relates to you as a cabin counselor. With the strong emphasis placed on the counselor as a key person for success, few camps traditionally included the cabin group and counselor as a teaching unit!

This might be expected, considering the historic influence of the centralized camping philosophy on Christian camps. The preacher and gifted teacher carried the Bible instruction load, since that's the way we did it back home.

Another problem plagued camps. That was the notion that if some Bible teaching was good, more was better. Let's visit a camp that I fear represents many!

More Is Better

The camp buildings nestled among the foothills of the Rockies, by a lovely, small lake. Towering firs surrounding the cabins. One wing of the dining hall served as the chapel. An attractive campfire circle was shaded by the firs.

Each day began with flag raising, with an added feature. A faithful pastor led brief morning devotions around the flagpole. His concept of *brief,* however, failed; and he marched the campers to the campfire circle to minimize their discomfort. While he warmed to his subject, the oatmeal grew cold and the cooks hot. But that was just the beginning of sorrows.

While still around the breakfast table the campers were presented with a missionary moment. The *moment* paralleled the *brief* of the flagpole speaker. Scarcely enough time remained to finish cabin cleanup before the first of two morning Bible classes began, not to mention the chapel hour with the visiting evangelist (my honor that week). Before the campers ever got to me they had had four gospel messages.

The afternoon was blessedly free until just before supper, when the bell summoned campers to another chapel gathering. I fail to recall the purpose, but perhaps it was singing and Bible memory time. And of course after supper little free time remained before the evening chapel (me again), and then a hurried trip to the canteen before a campfire service. The final touch was cabin devotions, the only time the counselors had with the campers all day!

If you kept score, you found five devotional/study sessions before lunch, one in the afternoon, and three after supper. That's nine inputs per day for six days, with no correlation between any of them. Is more always better?

Some would challenge the suggestion that these campers suffered an injustice. After all, isn't Bible camp the place where the Bible should be taught? But there's a whale of a gap between talking and learning!

AN ALTERNATIVE VIEW

Let's visit another camp, serving about the same number of

junior campers. At flag raising the flag was raised with respect, and at breakfast a hot meal was served with dispatch. Then the campers raced to their cabins for morning chores, to be followed by cabin Bible study. The counselor, who would become their best friend at camp, led the study.

But it wasn't really a study. It was more like an adventure, an exploration. Together the campers and counselor read the account of Jesus calling Peter, Andrew, James and John. Every camper knew the story, but it was fun to read it again. The counselor looked around the circle.

"Why do you suppose God put this story in Luke?" she asked. "What do you think He wanted people to learn?"

The answers were brief and simple. There was some giggling and play. The counselor kept leading her campers back into the story, hinting at ideas, asking question. She had them read in unison Luke 5:11, "And when they had brought their ships to land, they forsook all, and followed him."

Thought by thought the counselor guided the girls through a familiar story, coming finally to Jesus' promise, "Fear not, from henceforth thou shalt catch men" (Luke 5:10). Throughout the session she sought to draw ideas from the girls, asking in conclusion, "What did the fishermen have to do before they could follow Jesus?"

"Bring their boats to land," responded a camper.

The girls sang two familiar choruses, "Fishers of Men," and "I have Decided to Follow Jesus." They passed a small box around the circle, each one drawing a folded paper and glancing at it, thus learning the name of her prayer mate for the day. They agreed to pray for a missionary who was visiting the camp, and for the cook who had sprained her ankle just before camp. The session ended, but the Bible study was just beginning.

Following lunch, all campers were required to return to the cabins for that unpleasant period called rest hour. But on each bunk the girls found a small folder bearing the title, *Camper's Log.* Inside they read, "Hello, camper! Welcome to Christ on the Seas." Brief instructions followed, outlining a pattern for Reflection Time.

The key verse shared during Bible exploration was there, and some think-it-over suggestions. Then came something called pray-back. The girls remembered that their counselor had explained that Christians can chat with God by talking to Him about a Bible verse; answering questions, claiming promises, seeking answers to puzzling statements, or just saying thank you to Jesus for His love.

The Camper's Log listed several suggestions for prayer, then left a line for the name of the day's prayer mate, another line for the special prayer work, and finally a line to jot ideas for sharing at cabin devotions.

The counselor moved from cot to cot, encouraging her campers as they practiced personal devotions, some of them for the first time in their lives. Each day the Bible exploration would be reinforced by this quiet time, with the question, "What does this Bibles story say to me?"

There was another daily Bible study, and chapel meetings and campfires through the week, but each speaker seemed to know about the stories of Christ on the Seas. And each speaker used the day's key verse somewhere in every lesson or message.

Then, when the camp was quiet and the lights were low, the counselor quietly began to sing, "I have decided to follow Jesus . . ." The girls joined in. They repeated the key verse together, most of them now from memory, since they had recited it several times through the day.

"Anything to share from today?" the counselor asked.

EXPLORE, REFLECT, SHARE

Several years ago I was helping camp leaders develop wilderness programs. The question of meaningful Bible study arose constantly. By combining the values of several approaches I synthesized the three-thrust approach described above.

Each day was built around one Bible passage, often a story from Jesus' ministry. One key verse from the story, or a related passage, was chosen. Time was set aside to explore the passage in the morning. Camper's Logs were prepared to guide afternoon personal devotions around the day's theme. Evening campfires focused on the day's happenings, and on sharing spiritual discoveries from the Bible exploration and quiet time.

With only minor adjustments, this Bible study pattern was employed in many resident camps with excellent results. The idea is worth considering, where some practical way has not been developed to involve the cabin counselor in Bible teaching.

Rather than adding further burdens to already overworked counselors, *Cabin/Trail Devotions* provide a framework for ministry through three sometimes-difficult cabin activities; group study, rest hour quiet time, and cabin devotions. The daily three-fold repetition, with review continuing through the week, assures retention of the key verse for most campers.

But is this enough Bible teaching for a camp genuinely committed to the proposition that Ted Ward's words are true? If the camp setting is the best possible environment for education, shouldn't more be attempted?

Remember that it is truth perceived and integrated into experience that constitutes education, especially Christian education. Remember, too, that the counselor spends more time with the campers than any other staff member. The Word of God is the agent of the Spirit. Doesn't it make sense to involve the counselor in Bible instruction, creating opportunity for spiritual conversation?

Chapel preaching and campfire testimonies are excellent means for sharing God's truth, but remember the limitations of the camper! Allow some time for reflection, and don't flood the mind with so many ideas that none can take root.

Cabin Trail Devotions

The counselor should enter wholeheartedly into whatever Bible study plan a camp follows, whether as a teacher or as a participant in study with the campers. The *Cabin/Trail Devotions* approach provides a framework for integrating three in-camp daily sessions, with a correlated, follow-up plan described in the next chapter. *Keep Climbing!* builds on the camp studies, and when a camp follows this plan, the counselor should become familiar with all materials to help the camper gain maximum value.

We have noted that only what a camper *learns* constitutes teaching. The exposure of a mass of materials has no value, except for the ideas that become part of the camper's thought.

Cabin/Trail Devotions present six Bible study passages, six key verses to memorize, and a three-fold approach to daily study and worship. One story and one key verse per day, viewed from three perspectives, assure some grasp of biblical truth, given an enthusiastic, dedicated counselor. Then a fourth dimension: *Keep Climbing!,* a 16-page, take-home follow-up manual with six studies paralleling the camp Bible study.

While Bible exploration may be led in several ways, the counselor remains the key for success in this camp Bible study plan. Here are the four parts of *Cabin/Trail Devotions.*

BIBLE EXPLORATION: An inductive study of the Bible passage and key verse, adapted to the age and maturity of the campers. This session sets the spiritual tone for the day.

REFLECTION TIME: Personal application of the Bible passage and key verse under the guidance of the counselor, following the Camper's Log. Four dimensions of prayer are taught.

CABIN DEVOTIONS: Sharing the days experiences and spiritual insights through brief devotions at bedtime. A review of the key verse in a devotional setting reinforces discoveries made through the day.

KEEP CLIMBING! Follow-up correlated with the camp Bible studies in a take-home, mail-back study, keeps the camp in touch with campers who have made decisions for Christ.

BIBLE EXPLORATION

The key word is *explore.* There's a difference between a guided tour and an exploration expedition, though both require a leader. The leader of a guided tour simply points out familiar landmarks as the group moves through. Explorers are looking for something new. There's room for both. But Bible exploration offers experience in digging out truths from the Bible, a skill vital to growth.

Ideally, the cabin counselor will lead Bible Exploration, though camp tradition or lack of counselor experience may require a teacher specialist. The counselor should be present during Bible Exploration. The leader must saturate him or herself with the Bible passage and key verse prior to camp to be prepared to lead the exploration expedition.

A Leader's Guide supplies brief background notes and discussion check points. The question to be asked is, "What does God say to the world in this story?" Through questions the campers are led to discover the central truths of the story and key verse. Prayerful leadership by the teacher/counselor makes this Bible study plan adaptable to any age and maturity level. Here are suggestions for leading Bible Exploration:

READ the Bible story and key verse carefully. Sing an appropriate hymn or chorus. **PRAY** for guidance in exploring the Scriptures.

GUIDE the search for spiritual truth, allowing meaningful digression, but controlling the flow of conversation. What is God saying through the Bible passage?

SUMMARIZE the principle ideas discovered by the group, suggesting important points missed.

REVIEW the Camper's Log. Teach and practice pray-back (talking the key verse back to God). Choose trailmates (prayer partners), select a prayer concern for prayer work. See the next section for additional information related to the camper quiet time.

TRUST the Holy Spirit to apply the Word to the campers. Watch for camper responses for personal conversation.

REFLECTION TIME

It's hard to imagine how any Christian can grow apart from a personal quiet time. Reflection time provides a simple pattern that can be continued when the camper goes home. The Camper's Log presents seven steps toward an effective quiet time. Young or immature campers will need guidance and supervision through the camp week. You will note that Reflection Time builds on the Bible exploration earlier in the day.

The traditional rest hour after lunch is ideal for Reflection Time. Each camper should be provided a Camper's Log and perhaps a pencil. The seven steps in Reflection Time are:

KEY VERSE: The verse is printed from the King James. Any version preferred by the camp can be used. The camper is encouraged to memorize each key verse, though repetition and review assure a grasp of the key verses as the camp period progresses.

THINK IT OVER: Encourage the practice of meditation, asking the question, "What does the key verse say to me personally?" Thoughts are suggested in the Camper's Log.

PRAY BACK: Discussing the Word with the Author. The camper will learn a valuable aspect of prayer overlooked by many Christians. Pray Back must be modeled for young campers, guiding them in talking over the Scriptures with the Lord.

YOUR OWN WORDS: Instruction in basic prayer. Teaching campers how to talk with God. Again, modeling and guidance will be helpful. We often fail to teach campers how to pray.

TRAILMATE: Exchanging prayer partners in the cabin, a new partner each day. The counselor should be included, and model Reflection Time each day for the campers, moving quietly among them to encourage participation.

PRAYER WORK: Sharing a prayer concern chosen by the cabin group each day; something simple and practical, a need that relates to the camp.

IDEAS FOR SHARING: Encouraging campers to jot down or keep in mind one or more thoughts from the Bible Exploration of Reflection Time to share during Cabin Devotions.

CABIN DEVOTIONS

Bible Exploration asks, "What does God say to the world?" Reflection Time asks, "What does God say to me?" Cabin Devotions asks, "What did God say?" The thoughts of the campers are turned once again to the day's key verse and the Bible story explored earlier. Opportunity is given to share thoughts and adventures from the day. Often God's Spirit will apply the Word to a camper's heart in the evening quiet.

No new ideas introduced, no search for a dramatic story, just the sharing of friends around an exciting day and a Bible story they have explored together. What better way to close the day than to say together the day's key verse, allowing its thoughts to echo in the camper's hearts?

KEEP CLIMBING . . . AT HOME AND BEYOND

Keep Climbing! offers a simple, workable, follow-up plan that carries the camper back through the experiences of his or her camp week. The key to success is the *Keep Climbing!* counselor, a person who takes seriously the spiritual purpose of Christian camping.

Keep Climbing! is a 16-page booklet with six mail-back Bible studies correlated with *Cabin/Trail Devotions.* The *Keep Climbing!* counselor reviews and returns the camper's work with a word of encouragement. Some campers will need nudging to follow through. Simple, easy to complete, *Keep Climbing!* builds on the week at camp, providing continued contact with a caring camp leader. Here are the four areas for follow-up study:

REMEMBER: References for each camp Bible study and key verse are listed. The Bible study and key verse are listed. The camper is encouraged to review the story and verse. Simple fill-in questions guide the camper back through the Bible study, and a memorable feature from the camp week is called for.

READ: A brief, additional Bible passage related to the camp study is introduced, with written responses requested. Again, the questions are simple, designed to teach rather than test.

REFLECT: The camper is asked to think about the camp study and new Bible passage, to pray it back to the Lord. Simple fill-in questions are asked.

RESPOND: Additional questions are listed to lead the camper into the Word and apply it to his or her life. Opportunity is provided to jot a note to the *Keep Climbing!* counselor.

Inexpensive, attractive teaching guides and campers' logs are available from Camping Guideposts, though camps may choose to develop their own materials. The *Keep Climbing!* booklet encourages campers who have made decisions to follow through immediately following camp.

However it is done, camp Bible study should have clear goals and a manageable content. Only what the camper carries home in his head and heart counts.

Leader's Guide

I. THE MIRACLE CATCH

Primary passage: Luke 5:1-11
Parallel passages: Matthew 4:13-17, Mark 1:16-20
Key verse: Luke 5:11

CHECK POINTS:

1. **What favor did Jesus ask?** Use of boat: push out from shore, steady the oars. Nothing dramatic. Peter might have said No. He was tired . . . fished all night. Discouraged . . . caught nothing. He was the leader . . . let Andrew do it!
2. **What unlikely command did Jesus make?** Push out . . . let down the nets. Wrong time . . . night was the time to fish. Wrong place . . . one fished near shore. Wrong commander . . . Jesus was a carpenter; Peter, the fisherman. Yet Peter obeyed! "Nevertheless, at thy word. . ." It pays to obey the word of God.
3. **What happened?** Two boatloads of fish . . . obedience made both Peter and his friends prosper.
4. **What effect did the miracle have on Peter?** Humbled himself . . . difficult for a proud man! Saw himself . . . "I am a sinful man." Humility and self acceptance; conditions for discipleship.
5. **How did Jesus respond?** Fear not! . . . a new peace. From now on you'll be catching men . . . a new assignment.
6. **How did the four respond to Jesus' invitation?** Beached their boats . . . left behind good things for better things.

THOUGHT STARTERS:

1. No one lives to himself. Peter's obedience brought blessing to others.
2. God provides for those who follow Him. Boats full of fish— the source of money for fishermen.
3. Jesus accepts sinful men when they acknowledge their sin. He uses sinners who accept His cleansing.
4. What boats might we need to beach to fully serve Him?

Camper's Log

I. THE MIRACLE CATCH—LUKE 5:1-11

Key verse: Luke 5:11 And when they brought their ships to land, they forsook all, and followed him.

Think it over: What does the Lord say to me in this Bible story? What do I remember from Bible exploration today?

Pray it back: Lord Jesus, those men left their boats and business to be with you to learn. They left everything! They brought their ships to land and forsook all. And they followed you. Am I doing that?

Your own words: What might you do to make your life more like Jesus? How can you be a better camper, more helpful to others?

Your Trailmate: _____

Prayer duty: _____

Ideas for sharing: _____

Things to remember:

Keep Climbing!

I. THE MIRACLE CATCH—THE CALL TO COMMITMENT

Remember: *The story: Luke 5:1-11. Key Verse: Luke 5:11*

Can you remember some ideas from the camp Bible study? Check yourself on the key verse. Repeat it several times. What about Peter, the fisherman, taking orders from Jesus, the carpenter? It always pays to obey Jesus' Word. In order to follow Jesus, what did the four fishermen do?

_____

Write the name of a special camp friend: _____

Read: Matthew 16:21-26. Key Verse: Matthew 16:24.

Jesus said that in order to follow Him a person must do three things. What are they? (Matthew 16:24).

_____

Reflect: Practice pray-back on Matthew 16:24 as you were taught in camp. Ask the Lord what it means to deny yourself, to take up your cross, and to follow Him. (You may want to ask your pastor or Sunday school teacher to explain this). Peter told Jesus He shouldn't think about dying. Why was it necessary for Jesus to die?

_____

Respond: 1. Jesus asked Peter to (Luke 5:3) _____

_____

2. Then Jesus asked Peter to row into deeper water and (Luke 5:4) _____

3. What happened? (Luke 5:6) _____

4. When Peter saw all the fish, what did he do and say? (Luke 5:8) _____

5. Jesus replied (Luke 5:10) "Fear not, _____

_____

6. Then what did the four fishermen do? (Luke 5:11) _____

_____

7. That was *commitment*. They gave up everything for Jesus so they could become His followers. Jesus said there were three things a person must do to become His follower. What were they? (Matthew 16:24)

_____

8. In your own words tell what you think this means for a Christian today:

9. Do you have questions or comments for your counselor?

Review Luke 5:11 and Matthew 16:24 again.

Cut out this page and mail it to your *Keep Climbing* counselor at the address on the back cover.

Date completed _____ Signed _____

Your address _____ City _____

State _____ Zip _____

11

Camper and Counselor Growth

Follow-up continues to be one of the most challenging aspects of Christian camping. So much rests on the relationship between the camp and its constituency. Denominational camps serve groups of churches that maintain contact throughout the year, helping greatly with follow-up. Christian agency camps have a similar advantage, in that they have a continuing program that relates the camp experience to group meetings back home.

The independent Christian camp faces greater problems, for campers come from many churches, or from unchurched homes. There is no simple, unfailing answer to the follow-up problem. The best hope lies with the cabin counselor, for he or she relates most closely to the camper, and has the greatest potential for building a relationship that can help the camper maintain the spiritual momentum gained at camp.

In Chapter Seven we reviewed the importance of follow-up, and some ways the counselor can minister beyond camp. Now we will consider the broader possibilities for the counselor, to conserve the spiritual gains of a week at camp.

CAMPER FOLLOW-UP . . . WHY BOTHER?

Night after night at camp, Jerry sat spellbound as a Christian layman shared his experiences. Jerry's admiration grew through several brief conversations with the speaker during the week. A man who would sacrifice potential wealth and fame for Christian principles deserved respect. The final chapel talk concluded with the call for commitment to Christ, and Jerry was the first to respond. He desperately wanted to know God as this man did.

The counselor's report stated that Jerry had been a good, responsive camper, and that he had registered a decision for life commitment. One copy of the report was filed with the camp, the other copy went to Jerry's home church.

The echo of Jerry's decision remained with him for several weeks, but he lacked the maturity and direction to follow through. His name lay buried in camp records, a number in the decisions-recorded section of the annual camp statement: *Life Commitments—374.*

No one knows what happened to the report mailed to Jerry's home church.

In another camp downstate, 11-year-old Lisa found herself in a cabin of strangers. She didn't know one person, and homesickness set in. Then she heard her counselor call, "Will you help me, Lisa?" The task was trivial, but Lisa felt the warmth of her counselor's interest. Homesickness fled.

At Thursday night cabin devotions Lisa spoke quietly, hesitantly. "Can anyone who wants to become a Christian? I mean, even someone who doesn't have a church?"

The answer was simple and clear. Lisa accepted the gift of life in Christ Jesus as her cabin mates looked on prayerfully. She packed for the trip home possessed by a joy greater than her few years had ever known.

Lisa's counselor wrote three brief paragraphs in her report. She mentioned Lisa's shyness, her evident lack of spiritual background, and her decision. "At cabin devotions Thursday evening, Lisa accepted Christ as Saviour. But she'll need lots of help."

One copy of the report went into the camp follow-up files. One copy was mailed to a church in Lisa's town—one that demonstrated its concern for young people. Lisa's name and address remained in her counselor's notebook, along with brief notations.

The week following Lisa's return home, a Sunday School teacher phoned. Would Lisa like a ride to church the next

Sunday? Would it be all right if a caller visited her home? Now Lisa had a church.

A month after camp closed, Lisa got a letter, a neatly mimeographed letter that went to all campers. But Lisa didn't get many letters. She prized this one!

Shortly before Christmas, the best letter Lisa ever got arrived, a bright, friendly note from her camp counselor. It closed, "I am praying that the Lord will help you grow in Him. And I hope you can come to camp again next summer. Maybe you'll be in my cabin!"

Christian camps have been accused of careless reporting because so little evidence is seen back home of the spiritual decisions claimed. A great part of this problem can be traced to the lack of a workable plan to help campers grow after commitments are made.

I think it's safe to say . . . either follow up or foul up. Decisions are not trivial matters.

"Follow-up? I don't let it frustrate me. We do the best job we can with the kids in camp, then we leave them to the Lord and the church back home."

That's one camp director's solution to the follow-up problem. But you can't help wondering if the Lord wouldn't appreciate a little help, especially for the kids who have no church back home.

The complexity of the problem is apparent in a newsletter from Camp Haluwasa in New Jersey. Director Charlie Ashmen wrote, "Around a campfire just a few nights ago, it was inspiring to see 80 to 90 percent of the campers dedicate their lives to the Lord. Pray that these commitments will be enduring and fruitful."

More than 1,000 kids ride the Haluwasa railroad to their cabins each summer. Camp Haluwasa is a remarkable place, and its campers come from all kinds of homes. Not even the most dedicated camp director can know each camper, let alone discover special needs that call for help after camp.

Is follow-up really necessary? If so, how much? And by whom? Where does the camp and the counselor fit into the total Christian community? The answer to these follow-up questions depends on many factors: the nature of the camper constituency, the location of the camp, and the level of support the camp can expect from the churches. But one answer seems to remain unchallenged. Unless the camp plugs its counselors into the follow-up program, the campers won't get much help.

THE FOLLOW-UP TEAM

The counselor can't handle follow-up singlehandedly, but he or she often does play a crucial role. Only the counselor relates to the campers in a way that allows discovery of the few in each cabin that need special help.

When a *camper's parents* are Christians, follow-up becomes part of family life. Mom and Dad will be eager to learn what happened at camp. They prayed for spiritual discovery for their youngster.

A large measure of the follow-up burden must be carried by *the home church,* for the camp and the church are one in purpose. The church that feels camp follow-up is busy-work hasn't discovered the meaning of Christian camping, or its immeasurable value to the church.

Too often *the camper himself* is forgotten as a member of the follow-up team. We'll mention campers helping one another later on. The camp should prepare a camper to help himself. The camp's attitude toward decisions and spiritual growth should be reflected in its teaching content, so the camper learns how to grow through personal Bible study, prayer, and Christian fellowship.

Follow-up is a team effort, but the best team needs leadership and a strategy. At the heart of this strategy lies the counselor who must be alerted to follow-up. The counselor's disciplined discernment and accurate reporting are indispensable to making any plan for personalized follow-up effective.

Overshadowing all follow-up strategy is the love of God for each camper. Christian camping operates on the premise that camps are but instruments God uses for His purpose. All spiritual ministry carries frustration, for leaders are in a hurry to move every person to the highest possible level. Yet spiritual growth that is real is hard won, both for the leader and the follower. Having done what he or she can, the camp director must leave the campers in the hands of the Lord.

Counselor Role in Follow-up

The counselor provides the key for most successes in camp. It's hard to imagine a workable follow-up system apart from an alert, concerned cabin group leader.

The personal touch makes follow-up work. Uninterpreted decision cards need not be ignored, but they may not mean much either. Taken together with a counselor's insights into the needs and attitudes of a camper, a decision card can mark a new beginning, one that should be followed.

With younger campers, the impact of a loving, hero-figure must be recognized. Youths quickly forget the awe with which a child views older persons. They forget, too, the romantic visions of camp, possibly a child's first extended stay away from home. Youngsters cherish the friendship of a counselor more than most older persons know, and the prospect of a letter in mid-winter will keep them searching the mailbox.

While the counselor-camper relationship changes as campers mature, the counselor is the only staff member who has the opportunity to become well acquainted with campers. Occasionally another leader will attract the confidence of campers, but the counselor's job places a major burden for follow-up on him or her.

Camper Reports

Most camps expect a written report from the counselor on each camper. Usually this will be submitted on a form, with copies to be mailed to the home church. Some camps file the reports for future reference.

Objective reporting includes the counselor's judgment of attitudes and responses, but suspicions of possible misconduct have no place. To give an opinion from observation may be highly useful. Comments like these might be written on the back of the evaluation form:

Mary (John) seems to know the right answers to spiritual questions and professes to know the Lord, but I feel she has a problem. She seemed inattentive during devotions and sometimes hostile when asked to fulfill duties. Several times I heard her talking down to campers who showed deep spiritual interests. She can give the date and place of her conversion, but I found no help from her in building a Christ-centered atmosphere in the cabin.

Mary (John) did not find it easy to give a testimony, but I noticed an unusual spirit of helpfulness. She frequently played games with smaller campers, and helped with cabin duties when it was not her responsibility. I noticed that she read her Bible more than most campers, and listened carefully during cabin devotions, even though she had little to say.

The complaint most commonly heard from church leaders about camper reports concerns the useless generalizations found on them. While it's comforting to know that Jeannie and Danny were happy campers, that's not much to work on.

It is possible that such a report reflects the truth. Not every camper experiences a major crisis at camp, nor should the counselor probe for something dramatic to report, when the week has been just a happy experience.

But crisis moments will come, and those who minister to the camper throughout the year should know about them. Conversions, commitments to church-related vocations, significant expressions of growth, these all belong on the counselor's report.

The counslor will never be expected to betray a confidence. Campers may share deep problems, to be kept only in the counselor's heart. On the other hand, the counselor should not hesitate to report attitudes or actions which reflect spiritual problems. The sullen, unresponsive camper needs help. The testimony-spouting camper whose actions belie his witness needs help too. Failing to report such information helps no one.

THE PERSONAL TOUCH

The camper report is a significant part of the follow-up program, but by no means the only effective approach. While the counselor must be realistic—a continuing correspondence with every camper isn't likely to succeed—there will be persons whose spiritual needs call for special effort.

Letters, a phone call now and then, occasionally a visit, can help this person survive. Referrals to Christians who live nearby, a note to the pastor in addition to the formal report, plus an extra measure of prayer by the counselor will lend further support to the camper.

Often persons with special needs come from homes which require caution. Parents antagonistic to Christianity will not help a youth who is seeking God's way. Aggressive follow-up by the best-intentioned Christian can cause much more harm than good. The counselor should seek to discover these circumstances, and spare the camper hardship by making contacts which will not alienate the home.

Counselor follow-up is more an attitude than a program. The formal report will be filed, and one or more of the follow-up approaches suggested in this chapter may be employed, but that extra measure of concern must come from the heart.

TEACHING CAMPERS HOW TO GROW

When you look at the average congregation, you must conclude that many Christians do not plan to grow. They exhibit little interest in personal Bible study, prayer, leadership, or Christian witness.

When people reach adult years, change rarely comes. While they go through the motions of churchmanship, they exhibit little enthusiasm. Occasionally a seasoned pew-warmer catches fire, but not often. The pattern established when one first becomes a Christian often sets the tone for the rest of life. The best possible counselor follow-up begins with the life-set of the camper. By example and precept, the counselor teaches campers how to look after themselves spiritually.

Some camps practice leader-centered devotions exclusively.

The counselor talks, reads, admonishes, and prays, while the camper listens. Discussion often means little more than reciting the answer to a leader's questions. Little opportunity is provided for the camper to exercise spiritual initiative.

The cabin setting offers an ideal atmosphere for practicing genuine worship. Practical prayer, honest inquiry into the meaning of a Bible passage, humble sharing of personal needs, mutual concern one for another; these are the ingredients of the growing spirit. Of course they will be adapted to the age and spiritual maturity of the group, but such teaching and practice will enable campers to go home with a sense of confidence. This is perhaps the counselor's greatest follow-up contribution.

FOLLOW-UP SUGGESTION

USING THE MAIL:

1. Send a brief note to each camper at least once between camp seasons. Make it warm, unpreachy, personalized by some reference to the camper's experiences at camp. When possible, mention a moment of special meaning in the camper's devotional life.
2. During a cabin group meeting (rest hour, rainy day, devotional period) request that each camper write *himself or herself* a note reporting experiences and resolves at camp. The counselor collects the letters to mail in mid-winter.
3. Draw names, or use some other appropriate means of exchange, and ask each camper to write a letter to another camper telling of the week's experiences, including spiritual objectives. The counselor collects the letters to mail at a later date.
4. Correspond with campers who have special needs, perhaps continuing the counseling begun at camp.
5. Have each camper write a letter to a friend, pastor, or parent to be mailed from camp sharing the camper's spiritual experiences and resolves.
6. Initiate a round-robin letter with address list enclosed.

Each camper adds his reflections on camp, sending it to the next on the list. The letter returns to the counselor who makes photo copies for every camper of the total letter.

USING THE PHONE:

1. Initiate a round-robin phone circuit during a specific season, having first circulated a phone number list. This is especially valuable in preparing for a winter retreat, utilizing evening phone rates.
2. Counselor hot-line: provide a phone number where campers can get help during periods of special need.
3. Once a year call each cabin member, offering encouragement and inviting the camper back to camp.
4. Call parents or pastor with a positive word concerning the camper's growth and spirit (often we report only problems).

MISCELLANEOUS:

1. Produce a tape cassette, similar to a letter, with each camper adding a few minutes of conversation.
2. Take a snapshot of cabin group, to be mailed to each camper with counselor's letter.
3. Organize a prayer-partner exchange for the year.
4. Circulate brief devotional books from one cabin member to another. (Allow one week or less per reader. Provide sturdy envelope mailer and address labels.)
5. Set up a correspondence study, corrected by the counselor.

FOLLOW-UP SPECIALIST'S ROLE

Camp leaders are beginning to recognize the value of engaging a staff person to specialize in camper follow-up. This person must possess unusual qualities, for follow-up quickly becomes tedious. A retired man or woman, whether lay person or pastor or missionary, who senses the spiritual potential of camping might fill the office.

When this person is a familiar camp personality, the follow-up ministry takes on added value. Impersonal form letters are better than nothing. A personal note, however brief, from a friend makes an impact.

A follow-up specialist might fill other assignments on the camp staff; a public relations person, visiting churches and pastors, maintaining good relationships with supporting churches is in itself valuable follow-up, for camp enthusiasm in the church increases the likelihood that a camper will return year after year.

The follow-up person might coordinate camp rallies in various areas, and assist in recruiting camp leaders. He or she might conduct training programs for counselors.

Correspondence study would appear on the surface to be ideal for follow-up. However, human frailties interfere. Often camps report disappointing results from such plans. Many campers register, accepting the study material. The first lesson comes back in goodly numbers. The second lesson falls off dramatically. By the third lesson, the project is abandoned.

Where correspondence study succeeds, the follow-up specialist proves his worth. He or she returns lessons promptly, with a note of encouragement. Reluctant students, are reminded, perhaps offering a small incentive for getting in the next lesson.

FOLLOW-UP AND CAMP BIBLE STUDY

Four girls sat with me as the chapel emptied one June evening at the Tanalian Bible Camp in Alaska. They had come to talk about the Lord. We read the Scriptures together, and each girl prayed to receive Christ as Savior, a blessed scene repeated thousands of times each year in Christian camps around the world.

I asked each girl to write in her Bible, *I received Jesus as my Lord and Savior tonight at the Tanalian Bible Camp*, then the date and her signature. I suggested that the girls tell their friends what they had done. I prayed for them.

Later I gave the girls' names to the camp leader and asked, "Now what happens?" With a touch of sadness he said, "They go home to a village where no missionary lives, and with no

Christian fellowship. Their homes are not concerned for the gospel. We only hope they will return to camp next summer."

This, too, is a scene repeated in thousands of camps each year, small camps led by volunteers, serving children from widely-scattered communities. It is not a matter of neglect or unconcern. We simply have not developed a simple, manageable plan for following up on decisions made in camp.

I lay awake long into the night pondering that problem. What could be done? We help children begin an upward course, how can we keep them climbing? I suppose the mountains surrounding the camp suggested the analogy.

I traced the camp experience backward to the first day. We had studied the Bible according to the simple plan outlined in Chapter Ten. Six verses had been memorized from Jesus' adventures on Galilee, six stories had been explored. Might it not be helpful if those verses and stories could go home with the campers, especially those who had made spiritual beginnings? The thought intrigued me. Before full daylight returned to the Alaska skies (it never gets really dark that time of year), a follow-up booklet took shape in my mind.

I called it *Keep Climbing!*, and it contained six studies based on the camp Bible discoveries. Each study carried the camper back over the camp experience, beginning with the Bible discovery. Simple questions were formulated to remind the camper of key ideas. Then a brief, new Bible passage was added, with another verse to remember. A few more questions were asked—teaching questions the camper could write out and mail to the *Keep Climbing!* counselor, a person committed to the ministry of follow-up.

There are many correspondence follow-up plans of course, and each serves well. *Keep Climbing!* is different in that it builds directely on the camp Bible study. It's an idea any camp could develop, given a little imagination and a few dollars.

The cabin counselor may or may not find it possible to follow the camper home with letters. A follow-up specialist needs a specific plan, one that allows the camper to be comfortable as he or she follows through. *Keep Climbing!* serves as the follow-up program for many camps today, and as a model for programs tailored to the Bible teaching plan followed by other camps.

It would seem to make sense to build follow-up on ideas taught at camp, particularly for young and spiritually immature campers. A sampling of *Get Ready!* is found at the close of Chapter Ten.

THE COUNSELOR'S GROWTH

We have considered the necessity for follow-up if the camper is to grow. Follow-up is equally important for the counselor, for the needs of camping never end.

The Christian who takes seriously God's claim on his or her life will likely discover some special ministry in addition to service in the church. Camp leaders pray for men and women with vision and commitment who will prepare for the demanding, rewarding work required for effective camping. Perhaps God's Spirit is leading you to become a Christian camping specialist.

We remind ourselves that camp is not an end in itself. Camping is a tool for spiritual work, an environment for spiritual discovery. Unless we keep this continually in our thoughts, camping will become little more than wholesome recreation. The heart of the leader is always more important than skill of hand or mind.

Let me warn you, however, that camping is addictive! Strange things happen to those who surrender to its mystique. The cost in time and energy can be considerable, and friends will wonder.

THE CHALLENGE OF CAMPING

Read the profiles of missionaries supported by your church. Note how many point to a camp as the place of conversion or calling to God's service. The next time a group of Christians gather, ask how many remember a special meeting with God at camp. Consider the children and youth in your church. Where did they make their commitments to Christ? You cannot escape the conclusion that camping is a place of harvest.

We have claimed that the strength of Christian camping lies in the cabin group led by a dedicated counselor. Yet without other program specialists—food service, business administrators, caretakers, speakers—camp would not be possible. The challenge of camping includes varied staff needs. As you grow in knowledge, you may find new leadership roles you can fill.

The challenge of camping lies also in its variety of forms. Biking, hiking, canoeing, climbing, sailing; almost anything campers enjoy outdoors can be utilized as camp program. Whether you serve a thousand in a camp chapel, or a half-dozen huddled around a campfire, the spiritual principles of camping apply. Whatever your gifts and skills, they can probably be used in camp.

For many, the challenge of the cabin group will be most compelling. It is the counselor who leads the camper into the program, and applies the spiritual might of camping to the heart of the camper through love, prayer, and wise leadership.

GROWTH IN CAMPING

Experience is always the best teacher, and determination will carry you through the trial and error beginning leaders inevitably suffer. But why not borrow the experience of others?

The final chapter lists helpful resources for personal study. A careful review of this book will lay a foundation for broader reading. Each author brings new perspectives to camping, offering additional insights. We have not discussed the camping skills which are adequately covered in program books. Read widely in the literature of Christian camping, and begin to build a personal camping library.

Growth comes through personal association as well as reading. Take part in training programs offered by your camp. Draw on the wider camping fellowship through conferences and workshops offered by your denomination, Christian Camping International, or the American Camping Association. Stimulating sectional, regional and national conferences for Christian camping leaders pool the experience of many for the benefit of all.

Personal membership in Christian Camping International and denominational camping associations will benefit you through the year. The *Journal of Christian Camping*, published by Christian Camping International (CCI) offers a wealth of camping information.

Almost every specialized camping interest has its magazine, whether wilderness camping, canoeing, skiing, biking or nature study. The public library is a resource sometimes overlooked by camp leaders. The Red Cross, YMCA and YWCA, Scouting, and Christian youth agencies often sponsor camp-related workshops.

The counselor's ultimate growth, however, comes as you apply insights and skills to practical experience. Make camp a part of your life by sharing in leadership each year.

EDUCATION IN CAMPING

Many Bible schools and Christian colleges have added camping courses to recreation or Christian education departments. The concluding chapter of *An Introduction to Christian Camping* (see Appendix) discusses this in depth. Perhaps a school near you offers such courses.

Young people looking to careers in church-related vocations should take camping courses, for camping serves almost every dimension of Christian service in North America and abroad. Camping on the mission field has been established for many years in some lands.

Universities and colleges offer a variety of programs in camping and outdoor education.

Some Christian schools operate camps. Wheaton College has provided leadership to educational camping through Camp Honey Rock, its Wisconsin Northwoods campus. Other schools conduct accredited programs at camps, and some camps have aligned themselves with Bible schools to provide credit for camp-sponsored educational programs.

Often young people fall in love with Christian camping and seek careers in that field. Unfortunately, the demand for career leaders is limited, though the need seems to be increasing. Many Christian agencies, however, employ camping specialists, who may serve in a variety of ways while heading up a camping emphasis.

GROWTH THROUGH CHURCH LIFE

The home church will always be the center of God's work in the world. Camps rely on churches for campers and for leaders. Camps often turn to churches for funds to build and expand facilities. Pastors fill key posts on camp boards and in camp leadership. Your home church offers a major resource for personal growth in camping.

You probably have recognized that the same attitudes and spiritual commitment required of a camp counselor belong also to the Sunday School teacher. Sharpen your skills in the church throughout the year.

Every church needs a camp booster. I referred earlier to Bible Camp Bill, one of my parishioners many years ago who brought the camp attendance trophy to our little church year after year. Camps can't minister to youngsters who don't attend! While some debate centers around the practical advisability of a counselor confining his or her services to youngsters from the home church, your presence at camp will be an encouragement to campers from home. Promoting camp attendance in your community will keep camping high on your prayer list.

Your presence in the church as a follow-up resource completes the circle. Camping is not a self-contained ministry. Only as the church and the camp work together can camping's full potential be realized.

UNIT 3

Appendix and Study Guide

The books, associations, and sources listed in this unit will point the reader to the broader field of materials important to growth in camp leadership. Since bibliographies so soon become obsolete, it was felt more helpful to identify sources that are kept current month by month.

The *Get Ready!* study guide will serve camps which request advance written responses from counselors. However, all who study the *Camp Counselor* will benefit from working through *Get Ready!* as a means of reinforcing key ideas from the text. *Get Ready!* is available separately from Camping Guideposts for camps that wish to train through correspondence, and that choose to loan copies of the *Camp Counselor* to trainees.

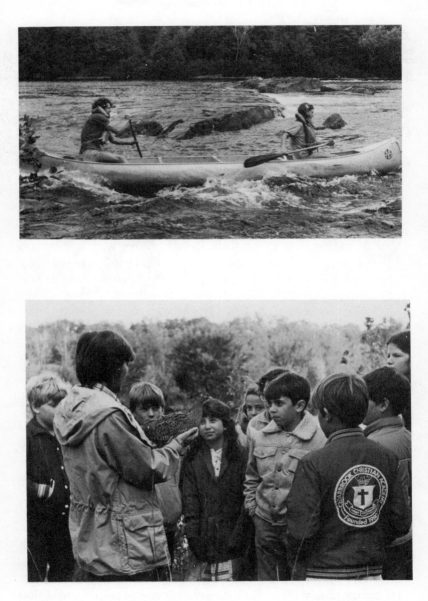

Appendix

The list of resources useful to a camp counselor is almost endless. Books dealing specifically with Christian camping are less numerous, but the alert reader can adapt information from many sources to grow in understanding and skill.

Two books belong in the personal library of all who are concerned about camp leadership. Both books include extensive bibliographies. A description of these titles appears below. They may be ordered through the Christian Camping International Book Service, Box 646, Wheaton, IL 60187. The CCI Book Service publishes a list of current titles that will acquaint you with a wide variety of available resources.

The American Camping Association, Bradford Woods, Martinsville, IN 46151, also publishes a booklist with helpful titles.

For a comprehensive overview of Christian camping, you should read *An Introduction to Christian Camping*, edited by Dr. Werner Graendorf and Lloyd Mattson, published in 1979 by Moody Press, 224 pages. This book was written by 13 camping experts and covers all aspects of Christian camping. It is the broadest discussion of Christian camping in print, with a thorough bibliography concluding each chapter. This book is avilable through C.C.I. or Camping Guideposts, $6.95

A long-time standard resource for general youth camping is the 572-page encyclopedia of outdoor skills and camping lore entitled *Camp Counseling*, by Mitchell, Robberson, and Obey; W. B. Saunders Co., publishers. The book may be ordered through C.C.I., and is worth the $22.95 cost. Probably the most complete listing of camping resources will be found in this book.

Denominational camping departments often distribute books and pamphlets of value. Don't overlook the public library. Your neighborhood bookstore carries many titles helpful to counselors, such as the Golden Nature Guides and the Peterson Field Guides.

Since the book market is so volatile, with titles coming and going, and with prices constantly rising, we will forego a list here, and refer you to C.C.I.

Every outdoor sport has one or more magazines, it seems. Government agencies release valuable outdoor brochures and booklets. Organization such as the Sierra Club and the Audubon Society publish authoritative books. For teaching about nature, a host of resources are available through publishers of outdoor education materials.

Camping Associations

Every active Christian camp leader should become part of *Christian Camping International,* a worldwide association of camp leaders. C.C.I.—Canada and C.C.I.—U.S. Serve more than 1,000 Christian camps and about 6,000 camp leaders. Student memberships are available, as well as personal membership for those who are no longer students. Schools, churches, and agencies hold membership, as well as camps.

C.C.I. sponsors conventions and workshops at area, district, regional, and national levels, bringing together camping experts from many nations. C.C.I. publishes the *Journal of Christian Camping,* a quality, bi-monthly magazine. C.C.I. puts you in touch with the Christian camping world, and opens a wide field of resources to help you grow as a camp leader.

The American Camping Association and the Canadian Camping Associations serve Christian camps in many ways, and are important sources for help to counselors. These associations sponsor conventions and workshops, and publish sound camping literature. A.C.A. publishes the bimonthly *Camping Magazine.*

Christian Camping International—Canada
745 Mt. Pleasant Road
Toronto, Ontario M4S 2N5
Canada

Christian Camping International—U.S.
Box 646
Wheaton, IL 60187

American Camping Association
Bradford Woods
Martinsville, IN 46151

Canadian Camping Association
Suite 2
1806 Avenue Road
Toronto, Ontario M5M 3Z1
Canada

CAMPING GUIDEPOSTS

Camping Guideposts, the publisher of this book, specializes in resources for leaders of Christian camps, with an emphasis on helps for the counselor. A quarterly newsletter is sent free to all who request it, with information on new releases and staff training. The following resources are available from Camping Guideposts; 5118 Glendale Street, Duluth, MN 55804.

The Camp Counselor, by Lloyd Mattson, 1981, revised, 1983.
   A 200-page counselor training manual.
Get Ready!, by Lloyd Mattson, 1981, revised, 1983.
   A 16-page study guide to the Camp Counselor, designed for correspondence study.
Introduction to Christian Camping, edited by Graendorf and Mattson, 1979, to be revised—1984.
   A 224-page overview of Christian camping, written as a textbook for Bible schools and colleges.

TRACK II Staff Training, by Lloyd Mattson.

Adaptation of *Introduction to Christian Camping* for advanced staff training.

Cabin/Trail Devotions, by Lloyd and Elsie Mattson, 1972, revised, 1982.

Bible study for camps; materials for the Bible class, camper quiet time, cabin devotions, and follow-up. Four titles: *Christ on the Seas*, *Christ on the Mountains*, *Straight Trails: Mark*, and *Elijah: Mountain Prophet*. Materials include Leader's Guide, Camper's Log, Keep Climbing! (follow-up guide), and program manual.

Good Morning, Lord! DEVOTIONS FOR MEN, by Lloyd Mattson, 1979, Baker Books.

Brief, pointed devotionals for men, programmed for use in men's retreats and staff training. Fifty devotionals.

Rediscover Your Family Outdoors, by Lloyd and Elsie Mattson, 1980, Victor Books.

Tips for family campers, 132 pages.

The Apples in the Seed, by Lloyd Mattson, 1983, 80 pages, Camping Guideposts.

The story of Camp Haluwasa, a remarkable Christian camp in the East.

Christian Outdoor Education, Barnett and Flora, 1982, 98 pages, Camping Guideposts.

Outdoor education for Christian schools and camps. An excellent introduction to an exciting program dimension for the camp and school.

Exploring God's Web of Life, Barnett and Flora, 1982, 80 pages. Camping Guideposts.

An excellent program guide for teaching outdoor education, useful in Christian outdoor education and summer camp programs. Studies of animal science, astronomy, atmospheric science, birds, insects, soil, trees and plants, and water conservation.

Guidepost—Camping Newsletter.

A quarterly newsletter for the camp director and staff trainer. Free on request.

Notes

Notes

Notes

Notes

Notes

Notes

Notes

Notes

Get Ready!

A Study Guide
to the

The Camp
Counselor

Lloyd Mattson

We see only what is,
God sees what is becoming.
Lord, as we serve campers,
Help us see like You.

Hello, Counselor!

Welcome to one of the greatest jobs on earth.

You're one of tens of thousands who serve campers each year. Most camp directors will agree that you are the key to success in camp. A good counselor is the camper's best friend.

You may feel a bit nervous, or downright scared. That's good. Scared people prepare. Preparation is more than half the battle, for when you're ready, you can concentrate on the campers.

Get Ready! is a study guide, not a test. Relax and work through the study units carefully. Camp counseling is mainly common sense, though some details must be mastered. Some of the information asked for in *Get Ready!* must be supplied by your camp through a *Camp Resources* packet. If this is not supplied, do the best you can from information in the *Camp Counselor*.

Use *Get Ready!* as a guide to the book and your camp resources. Scan all the study units to learn the kinds of information you're looking for. Then mark your book as you read, identifying the paragraphs that provide answers for *Get Ready!*

Add your comments and questions to each study unit. Should the philosophy or procedures of your camp differ from those of the *Camp Counselor,* go with your camp's viewpoint.

Study prayerfully. What you are is always more important than the information or skills you possess. The *Camp Counselor* and *Get Ready!* were written with the prayer that you will find joy in the vital ministry of camp counseling.

Lloyd and Elsie Mattson
Camping Guideposts
Duluth, Minnesota

1. Backgrounds To Christian Camping

Read:

Camp Counselor: Chapters 1 and 2.

Camp Resources: Counselor job description, staff training program, organization chart. Questions to be answered from this material are marked with an asterisk*.

Reflect:

Christian camping has enjoyed a long and dramatic history as a vital part of the gospel outreach. You become part of nearly 200 years of ministry in the outdoors as you serve your campers. What you are is far more important than what you will learn through this study. Tune your heart as you train your mind and body. You can make an eternal difference for some at camp.

Respond:

1. List three foundations and four tools for effective counseling identified in Chapter 1. _____

_____

_____

2. In your opinion, what marks a camp as *Christian*? _____

_____

* 3. Summarize the counselor job description. What does your camp require? _____

_____

_____

* 4. To whom will you be responsible in the camp management structure? _____

_____

5. From Romans 12, list the qualities that equip you to be a good counselor. _____

_____

6. How do you plan to maintain your spiritual vitality under the pressures of camp? _____

_____

* 7. Where will you turn for help should problems arise that you can't handle? _____

8. Write a brief statement listing the reasons why you have applied to be a camp counselor. _____

_____

_____

_____

_____

_____

Questions or Comment:

2. Serving Your Cabin Group

Read:

Camp Counselor: Chapters 3 and 10.
Camp Resources: Camp philosophy, discipline procedure, Bible study, camper quiet time, and cabin devotions plan.

Reflect:

This unit discusses your role as a cabin group leader. Here you will find your greatest challenge and opportunity. Read thoughtfully and prayerfully the chapters from *Camp Counselor* and related Camp Resources. Much of the value your campers gain from camp depends on how well you master this unit.

Respond:

1. List the characteristics of the age group you will serve during your counseling period(s). _____

_____

_____

2. What do you think is meant by "the camper's moment of discovery," sometimes called the teachable moment? _____

_____

_____

3. How does the moment of discovery concept affect your work as a counselor? _____

_____

_____

* 4. Describe the discipline policy followed in your camp.

_____

_____

_____

5. Identify three basic elements found in effective cabin devotions. _____

_____

6. What are the elements in good cabin etiquette? _____

_____

7. Describe the *Cabin/Trail Devotions* Bible study plan outlined in Chapter 10, and tell how you would prepare to lead such a study. _____

_____

_____

_____

_____

_____

_____

_____

8. What steps would you take to manage your cabin the first night of camp? _____

_____

_____

Questions or Comment:

3. Serving The Whole Camp

Read:

Camp Counselor: Chapters 4 and 5.
Camp Resources: Review camp philosophy, nature study opportunities, health and safety standards,
emergency procedures.

Reflect:

This study unit concerns your relationship to the total camp
program. While you are responsible primarily for your cabin
group, you become an important part of the leadership team
as you take part in all-camp activity. You may possess skills
that can enrich camp for everyone. Your spirit and willingness to serve where needed—without intruding into the responsibility of others—will strengthen other staff members.

Respond:

1. How might a counselor make meals a pleasant time?

_____

_____

_____

2. In what ways can the counselor make all-camp worship
and study more effective? _____

_____

_____

* 3. What responsibilities will you have beyond your cabin
groups? _____

_____

_____

* 4. What nature study opportunities are provided by your camp? _____

_____

_____

5. In your opinion, what values might a camper gain from nature study and campouts? _____

_____

6. Name three activities you could lead on a rainy day.

_____

_____

_____

* 7. What procedure would you follow in the event that one of your campers became injured or ill? _____

_____

8. How would you help a homesick camper? _____

_____

_____

9. What is your role should a serious accident occur?

_____

_____

_____

* 10. Describe the evacuation and search and rescue plan for your camp. _____

_____

_____

_____

11. How can you promote wholesome boy-girl relationships in camp? _____

_____

_____

Questions or Comment:

4. Counseling The Individual

Read:

Camp Counselor: Chapters 6 and 9.
Camp Resources: Evangelism plan, procedure for recording decisions, referral persons, follow-up plan.

Reflect:

Counseling the individual is the ultimate privilege of the counselor. If life is the product of its choices, then skill in guiding campers in making choices should be given priority in the counselor's preparation.

Respond:

1. The heart and the ear are described as the most important parts of the counselor's anatomy. In your opinion, what does that mean? _____

_____

_____

_____

2. When is the best time to lead a camper to Christ? _____

_____

* 3. Describe how you would lead a camper to Christ for salvation. _____

_____

_____

_____

_____

4. What would you say is the goal of the counselor when a camper comes with a problem? _____

_____

_____

* 5. How would you help a camper who came to you with a problem you felt was deeper than your counseling skill could handle?_____

_____

_____

6. How can you help a camper build his or her spiritual life after a decision is made? _____

_____

_____

7. Why is it more important to base a camper's decision on the Scriptures than on your advice or persuasion? _____

_____

_____

_____

* 8. What record does your camp require you to make of camper decision? _____

_____

_____

Questions or Comment:

5. Wrap-Up And Follow-Up

Read:

Camp Counselor: Chapters 7 and 11.

Camp Resources: Camper report procedure, camp evaluation forms, follow-up program, staff growth opportunities.

Reflect:

What happens after camp may be as important to the camper as the camp experience. This study unit concerns reports, evaluations, camper follow-up, and your personal growth.

Respond:

* 1. What evaluations will be expected of you following camp? _____
_____

_____

2. What preparation can you make through the camp period to write a useful camper report? _____
_____

_____

* 3. What information should you include in the camper report? _____
_____

_____

4. Chapter 7 lists 20 questions for self-evaluation. How might these be used in your preparation for counseling?

_____

_____

_____

* 5. What is the follow-up plan employed by your camp?

_____

_____

_____

6. Name several ways a counselor might share in camper follow-up. _____

_____

_____

_____

7. A Bible study plan which includes follow-up is described in chapters 10 and 11. What advantages do you see in the *Keep Climbing!* idea? _____

_____

_____

_____

_____

8. What steps might you take to grow in camp leadership?

_____

_____

_____

_____

9. What relationship do you see between the camp and the church? _____

_____

_____

_____

Questions or Comment:

6. Sharpening The Focus

Read:

Camp Counselor: Chapters 8 and 12.
Camp Resources: Camp goals and objectives, staff growth opportunities.

Reflect:

When we stop growing, we start dying. That is true for institutions as well as individuals. This unit looks into refining goals for the camp, the camper, and the counselor. Resources for growth are listed.

Respond:

1. Chapter 8 applies the story of the raising of Lazarus to the ministry of camp. Name the three commands Jesus gave, and tell how you think they might apply to camp. _____

_____

_____

_____

_____

_____

2. How big should a camp become? _____

_____

_____

3. What are the fundamentals for Christian growth? _____

_____

_____

_____

4. A personal devotional plan is outlined in Chapter 8. Briefly describe it, and suggest some values. _____

_____

_____

5. What is the grand Christian alibi, and why is it wrong?

_____

_____

_____

_____

* 6. List several ways you can grow in effectiveness as a camp counselor. _____

_____

_____

_____

7. Now that you have completed *Get Ready!*, how do you feel the study had helped you? What information did you find lacking in the *Camp Counselor* of your Camp Resources Packet? _____

_____

_____

_____

_____

Questions or Comment:

Name _____ Date _____

Address _____ Phone _____

City_____ State/Province _____ Zip/Postal Zone _____

I'm Ready!

No one is ever completely prepared for camp, for the unexpected inevitably arises. But you can be prepared for the expected! Here is a check list. See how you measure up.

I am ready spiritually:

_____ My devotional life is in tune.

_____ I pray for camp and my campers often.

_____ I've chosen a Bible verse to live with through camp.

I am ready mentally:

_____ I have studied all materials supplied by my camp.

_____ I have carefully read the *Camp Counselor*.

_____ I have completed *Get Ready!* and other required training materials.

I am ready physically:

_____ I have gathered equipment, personal effects, appropriate clothing, and other materials needed for counseling.

_____ I have arranged to reach camp on time, and leave only after all my responsibilities are cared for.

_____ I have notified the camp director of physical limitations that might affect my service.

I am ready specifically:

_____ I understand my responsibilities as a counselor and part of the all-camp team.

_____ I have completed preparations to the degree possible at this time.

Name _____

ollow the instructions
ed to mail your work
staff training session.

ristian camping lead-
who found our materi-
s strengthen Camping
d. Write to us at the

d and Elsie Mattson
ping Guideposts
5118 Glendale Street
Duluth, MN 55804

Camping
Guideposts